"Nothing brings me greater joy than sharing the life-changing message of Jesus Christ with individuals…and equipping others to do the same. For that reason alone I am thrilled to see this book in print. Dale is a champion when it comes to discipleship, and his heart for the lost beats closely with mine. Pick up this book, dig in, and use it to learn how you can truly become an active participant in God's Great Commission."

LUIS PALAU // Evangelist and Author

"paradigm-shifting"

"Some will say the better way described in this book is a rehash of old ideas. It is not. Dale Losch is describing a paradigm-shifting reorientation of how we do mission. The seismic geopolitical and technological shifts that are making the world smaller and faster have simultaneously closed many doors for traditional missions and opened many doors for Christ-followers in the marketplace. I will be cheering for Crossworld and others who are bold enough to explore this 'blue ocean' opportunity for accelerating the fulfillment of the Great Commission."

STEVE MOORE // President, Missio Nexus

"Missionaries, pastors (and I speak as one who has been a pastor for 32 years), and above all those of you who consider yourself 'just a lay person'—this book is a must-read. I have had the added privilege of knowing the author for several years. And I can vouch for the fact that he personally practices what he advocates in this book."

SUNDER KRISHNAN // Senior Pastor,
Rexdale Alliance Church, Toronto

"remarkably accessible"

"If there is a better way to reach the world, then this is it. Maybe it is the original way, for it is ordinary people, in ordinary places, doing ordinary things with extraordinary results—for their vision at work, home and play is to participate in the church's greatest task: making disciples of Jesus Christ. This book shows it to be a remarkably accessible task for all those who belong to Christ. Enjoy the adventure."

CHARLES PRICE // Pastor, The Peoples Church, Toronto
Host of Living Truth Television and Radio

"mission classic"

"My heart leaped within me as I read Dale Losch's *A Better Way*. It will become a mission classic as it is building much-needed bridges between the workplace movement, Business as Mission, traditional missions, and the local church. The clarity in which he defines discipleship is worth the whole read. Read it and do it! Dale Losch's *A Better Way* shows us how to return to the biblical model of Jesus in fulfilling the Great Commission."

KENT HUMPHREYS // Ambassador, The Fellowship of Companies for Christ International / Christ@Work

"In *A Better Way*, Dale Losch boldly and honestly addresses the challenges of our current strategy for reaching the least-reached of the world. He then paints the picture of how this generation can make disciples of every nation. This is a must-read for everyone who is serious about the Great Commission."

DURWOOD SNEAD // Director of globalX, North Point Ministries

"must-read"

"I have found *A Better Way* by Dale Losch to be the most meaningful book on missions I have read in a long time. I will be praying for the missionaries with Crossworld to be ready to make this vision a reality. [Crossworld is] right in the middle of the beginning of a mission that could dramatically change the vision of every evangelical mission in America!"

DR. NEIL ASHCRAFT // Minister-at-Large, Dallas Theological Seminary

Share your thoughts

What do you think about A Better Way *by Dale Losch?*

Your name ______________________________

City ____________________ **State/Province** __________

Occupation ____________________ **Age** __________

Your thoughts:

Capture an image of this page with your smart phone, camera or scanner and send it to abetterway@crossworld.org. Your thoughts may be selected to appear in Crossworld's promotional efforts.

☐ Use my comments with only my first name and location.

☐ Use my comments, but keep my name and location anonymous.

Share this book

Keep the message of A Better Way *moving by passing this book to a friend.*

Share your thoughts

What do you think about A Better Way *by Dale Losch?*

Your name ____

City ____________________________ **State/Province** __________

Occupation __________________________ **Age** ______________

Your thoughts:

Capture an image of this page with your smart phone, camera or scanner and send it to abetterway@crossworld.org. Your thoughts may be selected to appear in Crossworld's promotional efforts.

- ☐ Use my comments with only my first name and location.
- ☐ Use my comments, but keep my name and location anonymous.

Share this book

Keep the message of A Better Way *moving by passing this book to a friend.*

Share your thoughts

What do you think about A Better Way *by Dale Losch?*

Your name ______________________________

City ____________________ **State/Province** __________

Occupation ____________________ **Age** __________

Your thoughts:

Capture an image of this page with your smart phone, camera or scanner and send it to abetterway@crossworld.org. Your thoughts may be selected to appear in Crossworld's promotional efforts.

☐ Use my comments with only my first name and location.

☐ Use my comments, but keep my name and location anonymous.

Share this book

Keep the message of A Better Way *moving by passing this book to a friend.*

Share your thoughts

What do you think about A Better Way *by Dale Losch?*

Your name ______________________________

City ____________________ **State/Province** __________

Occupation ____________________ **Age** __________

Your thoughts:

Capture an image of this page with your smart phone, camera or scanner and send it to abetterway@crossworld.org. Your thoughts may be selected to appear in Crossworld's promotional efforts.

- ☐ Use my comments with only my first name and location.
- ☐ Use my comments, but keep my name and location anonymous.

Share this book

Keep the message of A Better Way *moving by passing this book to a friend.*

Share your thoughts

What do you think about A Better Way *by Dale Losch?*

Your name ______________________________

City ____________________ **State/Province** __________

Occupation ____________________ **Age** __________

Your thoughts:

Capture an image of this page with your smart phone, camera or scanner and send it to abetterway@crossworld.org. Your thoughts may be selected to appear in Crossworld's promotional efforts.

- ☐ Use my comments with only my first name and location.
- ☐ Use my comments, but keep my name and location anonymous.

Share this book

Keep the message of A Better Way *moving by passing this book to a friend.*

A BET-TER WAY

MAKE DISCIPLES WHEREVER LIFE HAPPENS

DALE LOSCH

KANSAS CITY, MISSOURI

A Better Way

Make Disciples Wherever Life Happens

Dale Losch

10000 N. Oak Trafficway, Kansas City, MO 64155, USA

Printed in the United States of America

ISBN-13 0-9656830-1-X

Cover and interior design by Tim Green.

Visit our website at crossworld.org.

CONTENTS

PREFACE

I am thoroughly captivated by the power of doing what Jesus told us to do. And I am thoroughly convinced that we need to get serious about it.

A Better Way is all about rediscovering the explosive power of Jesus' disciple-making mandate to all believers. It's about unleashing the untapped potential of the whole body of Christ. It's about innovatively using one's profession to launch disciple-making communities in the world's least-reached marketplaces. But more than anything, it's about the very heart of God longing for mankind to rediscover life as it was meant to be—life to the full. This book is not about discovering a *new* way, but about recovering a *lost* way—Jesus' way of bringing soul-satisfying life to the world.

A Better Way is for believers who want to get in the game like never before—not just as "payers and prayers" but as *players* among the world's least-reached people. It's for churches who recognize the futility of filling pews with converts, and instead want to fill the world with disciple-makers. It's for classical "missionaries" like me, who believe there is a crying need for disciple-makers from all professions to come join them in the harvest. And it's for those who have tasted life as it was meant to be—abundant life, life to the max—and cannot fathom keeping it to themselves.

A Better Way is an invitation to join in the pursuit of a dream—a dream of *disciple-makers from all professions bringing God's love to life in the world's least-reached marketplaces.*

CHAPTER 01

IS THERE A BETTER WAY?

"I want to impact the world for Jesus, but I don't want to do it your way."

My twenty-two-year-old son Joel had just spoken into my world, but I'm not sure I was listening. After all, he was fresh out of college and right at the front end of figuring out life.

He was idealistic. I was realistic.

He was adventuresome. I was grounded.

He hadn't even landed his first "real" job yet. I had just been named the president of Crossworld, the missionary-sending organization that my wife and I had joined twenty years earlier.

Joel would learn soon enough that the well-worn tracks of the so-called modern-day missionary movement, carved into the soil by godly men and women over the past two hundred years, were in fact tried and true and worthy of his allegiance as well.

My wife, Jerusha, and I first sensed God nudging us toward cross-cultural ministry in 1986 during my third year as a student at Dallas Theological Seminary. Until then, I had my sights set on pastoral ministry in Canada. To be honest, for most of my life I had held a rather low view of missions and of missionaries, and had never aspired to be one myself. I had concluded, quite erroneously, that missionaries were some sort of second-string religious workers not quite sharp enough to serve as pastors in the North American church. Instead they were sent overseas where requirements and expectations were not as high.

God began to nudge me using, among other things, the powerful preaching and teaching of a number of great missionary communicators. One was a man by the name of George Murray, whose message from Luke 15 on the prodigal son I remember to this day. Speaking to some eight hundred seminary students gathered in the hallowed halls of Chafer Chapel, he said, "Many of you say that you are willing to go, but you're planning to stay. Maybe more of you should be planning to go and willing to stay."

That moment marked the beginning of my own journey to the nations. By my final year of seminary, Jerusha and I had settled on France as our future destination and on Crossworld as the missionary-sending agency that would get us there. We attended Crossworld's four-week training for new missionaries, raised $3,000 in monthly financial support, and boarded a plane for France. We were full-time vocational missionaries just one year after graduation.

Now, twenty years later, my firstborn son, who had made that journey to the nations with his parents as a two-year-old child, was telling me he wanted to make that journey again but didn't want to travel the same path we had. He didn't want to go to seminary, apply to a mission organization, raise support, and become a vocational religious worker. He wanted to make a real difference in the real world by getting a "real job." Not that my job wasn't real, but it certainly wasn't typical.

I wasn't the least bit hurt or threatened by my son's desire to forge a different path. I knew he loved and respected us in our missionary vocation and was not passing judgment on our way. He just wanted to find a different way. But I was frustrated—not so much by his desire as by my own inability as the leader of an organization committed to impacting the world for God's glory to offer a pathway to people like my son.

Joel is not alone. He represents a vast, largely untapped source of godly people—both young and old—who want to make a difference for Jesus in this world without having to follow the worn and often rutted paths of the missionary movement as we have known it. Dare we admit, even believe, that there is another way, a different way, maybe even *a better way*, to engage the lost world for the glory of God? In time, I have come to believe that there is. But it took some serious thinking and questioning for me to see it.

Dare we admit, even believe, that there is another way, a different way, maybe even *a better way*, to engage the lost world for the glory of God?

How could any call be higher than to leave a secular profession to serve God full time as a vocational Christian worker? What could possibly be better than going off to a Bible-training institution to get a specialized ministry degree? What better way is there to fund genuine missionary ministry than to raise support? How could anyone improve on the church-planting vision that has been the mainstay of missionary activity for much longer than I have been around? Who could possibly suggest a better way to accomplish the Great Commission than to send long-term, fully-supported, seminary-trained preachers, teachers and evangelists to proclaim the gospel and build the church?

Some will undoubtedly be offended by the mere suggestion that there may be "a better way" to offer Jesus to the world, seeing it as an affront to former ways. Yet is it not Jesus who is *the* Way, the source of abundant life as it was meant to be? Is He not worth our undying effort to continually seek the very best ways to offer that life to others?

To keep on doing things the way we've always done them when the world and its people have so drastically changed is both naïve and arrogant.

Audacious as it may sound, I believe there *is* a better way to offer life to the world as we look to the future, and I am committed to discovering it.

That is not to say that people have been doing it all wrong. When I see a vibrant church of four hundred fervent believers in Milan, Italy, worshipping God and seeking to extend His kingdom, it's obvious that we've done something very right. When I read the stories of the generation that preceded mine, spending a lifetime reaching stone-age animists and seeing them turn to Christ by the tens of thousands, my heart longs to be so used of God. They must have done something *very right.*

In the past hundred years, we have witnessed some of the greatest kingdom progress since the initial advance of the gospel made by the first-century church. The spread of the gospel in places like South America over the past century is mind-boggling. In 1900, evangelical believers on that continent numbered roughly 700,000, or 1 percent of the population. By the year 2000, the number of believers exploded to 55 million, or 11 percent of the population.

Sub-Saharan Africa has witnessed similar growth. In 1900, there were an estimated 1.6 million believers, while today the number stands at more than 116 million.

The growth of the non-Western evangelical missionary force has been another cause for celebration. During that same hundred-year period, the number of cross-cultural workers from non-Western countries increased from about 250 to an estimated 180,000. Today, non-Western workers outnumber their Western counterparts by more than three to one.

To say that there is a better way is in no way an indictment of the former ways. Rather, it's a recognition that the world today is a vastly different place than it was even twenty years ago. The migration of nations, the rise of a global missionary force, the rapid growth of urban populations, the development of a global economy, the explosion in technology, and the restriction on religious activity in many countries are just a few of the realities that demand a reexamination of our model.

To keep on doing things the way we've always done them when the world and its people have so drastically changed is both naïve and arrogant—naïve to assume that the same approach in a radically different context will continue to work, and arrogant to assume that we have no need to learn and grow in our approach to making disciples of all nations.

CHAPTER 02

MEET YOUR NEW NEIGHBOR

There's a new family in your neighborhood and they're from Saudi Arabia. They don't speak much English, but they seem eager to get to know you in spite of the language barrier. You're not so sure about the prospect of your neighborhood becoming ethnic and the potential impact that will have on house values. But these folks seem nice enough and apparently have sufficient resources to buy into the neighborhood. In fact, unlike many immigrants who seem to arrive in our cities with meager means, this family seems quite middle-class. They even drive an SUV like many of your other neighbors.

The strange thing is, you never see them going to work. While everyone else on your street leaves for work in the early morning, the Saudis, as you've come to refer to them, don't seem to come and go at normal hours.

One Saturday while you're out mowing the lawn, you notice "Mr. Saudi" in his front yard doing the same. So you decide to take a break and go meet him. "Good morning! Welcome to our neighborhood!" you exclaim. The conversation stumbles along between his broken English and your increasingly loud attempts to communicate with simple words and hand gestures. Finally you get to ask him what you've been wondering ever since he moved next door: "What do you do for a living?" To which he calmly replies, "I'm a missionary."

A missionary! You hope the shock hasn't registered on your face. A Muslim missionary has moved in next to you!

Think about it. How would you feel if this scenario actually played out in your world? If he were an engineer, an oil executive or even a taxi driver, it would be one thing. But a *missionary*? As a believer, you might see this as a unique opportunity to influence him for Christ, but for the average person, this would feel like a serious threat.

I don't know how my neighbors in France felt when they first discovered that a missionary had moved in next door to them. I do know they were curious and slightly offended that Americans thought the French even needed missionaries (as though they were poor or needy). They often asked what a Canadian-American couple like us was doing in their town of sixteen thousand people. Other questions were left unspoken. Why did our car not leave the parking lot at 8 a.m. every morning like everyone else's? How can anyone with a two-year-old child afford to live in their country without apparently working? Where did our money come from?

I will not hide that it was a real challenge to face the inevitable question, "What do you do for a living?"

I will not hide that it was a real challenge to face the inevitable question, "What do you do for a living?" How could we explain to them that I was a Protestant pastor, paid by American churches to come and start a church in their town where there was already a Catholic church in every neighborhood? The truth is, it doesn't really matter what the neighbors think when one is sent by God. Some level of defensiveness is to be expected. But is it possible that some of the defensiveness and suspicion could have been avoided had I not had a "missionary" status?

Fast-forward to the year 2011. The city is Dongguan, China. The new neighbor is a twenty-five-year-old single guy from Canada by the name of Joel. My son Joel. The same Joel who wants to impact the world for Jesus but does not want to do it the same way his parents did. So how is *he* doing it?

Upon graduating from a university with a degree in international business, he worked as a waiter for eight months while he tried to figure out what he would do next. Then, with his savings and a little financial help from family and close friends, he moved to China. He spent ten months there learning Mandarin and investigating business opportunities. He then returned to Canada where he picked up another job as a waiter and began looking for a position with a Canadian company that did business in China. A few months later, he was back in China working as a purchaser for a manufacturing company based in Toronto.

What do Joel's Chinese neighbors think of him? I'm sure they are curious, perhaps even puzzled, that a young guy would choose to leave a country like Canada to come to their megacity. They may wonder whether he has a girlfriend, how much money he makes, or how long he plans on staying there. But when he walks out the door at 6:30 a.m. every morning to catch the company shuttle that will take him across the city to work, they understand that he spends most of his day doing something very similar to what they do.

There are a lot of things that Joel doesn't have that his parents had twenty-two years ago. He doesn't have the freedom to give his full-time attention to religious work. He doesn't have a team of like-minded believers to work with and keep him focused on spiritual outcomes. He doesn't have the support structures of a mission organization to help him with loneliness, cultural adjustments and language learning.

At the same time, Joel has a number of advantages that my wife and I never had when we began our ministry—immediate, natural bridges of relationships in the office, a rapid mastery of the language that comes from immersion in the working world, a visa that allows him to freely live and work there and, in the case of China, freedom to speak about his faith in Christ without the risk of being expelled from the country.

How could anyone possibly do missionary work while working fifty hours a week in the business world?

But how does he find time for ministry? How could anyone possibly do missionary work while working fifty hours a week in the business world? What mission organization would accept him as one of its members when he has no seminary training, no sending church, no financial ties to the organization, and no ability to give himself to full-time ministry?

These questions need careful consideration. But before dismissing Joel's way as a potential model for ministry, we need to find out if there is a way to wed the advantages of both models, creating a new model that would engage the whole body of Christ in a better way that suits the world in which we live.

CHAPTER 03

MOBILIZING ALL BELIEVERS

Joel is not a church planter—at least not in the commonly understood way of defining it. He's only twenty-five years of age. He lives by himself, spends twelve hours a day at work, and comes home mentally and physically tired.

But Joel loves Jesus. He reads God's Word daily. He prays for the lost and seeks to share his faith in word and deed. He has a passion for life and for making a difference. He represents an incredible, largely untapped potential for transforming the world in our lifetime, if we are willing to believe that there is a better way. But first it is necessary for us to recognize that we have actually stood in the way of unleashing that potential.

I met Darryl and Rosa in 2010 at a missions conference. They are in their early forties and have worked in the professional world since finishing graduate school. They've also been heavily involved in leading Bible Study Fellowship groups for years. Having immigrated to the U.S. from a Hispanic culture, Rosa has extensive cross-cultural experience. Both Darryl and Rosa struck me as mature, godly people.

As I interacted with them, it was clear that they both had a strong interest in serving God cross-culturally. So I told them about Crossworld's ministries and encouraged them to connect with their church leaders to seek their input and support. (I strongly believe the local church should play a central role in the process of sending cross-cultural workers.)

Since that initial contact with them, we've connected several times by phone and email. I have encouraged and counseled them in their pursuit of God's place for them. But recently I received an email from Darryl that illustrates why we are sometimes guilty of standing in the way of unleashing believers to reach the world. He wrote, "In speaking with the pastor regarding mission work, he has indicated that I would need to have formal seminary training to be supported by our church. In all honesty I do not see this for me at this point in my life, and I trust God that the gifts He has given me are effective for the mission field."

Now I have nothing against seminary training. My years at Dallas Theological Seminary were outstanding. Nor do I advocate sending people into battle unprepared. Solid biblical training and experience is critical. Yet it seems to me that when a godly, mature, ministry-rich couple is required to go to seminary before the church will send them to impact the nations, there is something wrong. There must be a better way.

HAVE WE COMPLICATED THE COMMISSION?

Just before Jesus left this world to return to His Father, He gave His followers a rather straightforward charge: go and make disciples of all nations. Though Jesus never gave it this title, His followers have come to refer to this charge as the Great Commission and have treated it with a sort of reverent awe. Churches developed what came to be known as missions conferences—annual events during which we pay special attention to the words of the Great Commission to reach the world for Christ. These conferences, lasting anywhere from a single Sunday morning service to one week, are generally dedicated to celebrating the work of those we honor as missionaries. We also try encouraging others to consider "the missionary call." Those who respond, generally few in number, subsequently quit their jobs, apply to a Bible-training institution, and spend the next several years studying the Scriptures and raising long-term funding for full-time ministry.

Even today, some two hundred years after the inception of what has been called the modern-day missionary movement, the average length of time from one's "call to missions" to actual deployment as a new missionary continues to rise. In April 2011 at a gathering of Great Commission organizations, one speaker claimed that it's taking five to seven years to deploy people once they've been recruited. For many, the journey is so long they lose sight of the "calling" and never make it.

We emphasize too often the product (the church) at the expense of the process (disciple-making).

For others the task is simply too daunting. The majority of those who have been sent out by the church and mission organizations over the past decades have been sent out as *church planters* entrusted with the task of *planting churches* and even starting *church-planting movements.* Many of those who sign up for this have never actually planted a church, much less a movement of churches in their own country. But they go, believing that God will enable them to achieve in a foreign culture what they have never actually done in their own. Others, unable to reconcile their lack of church-planting experience with the stated task, simply don't go at all.

I'm not suggesting that we abandon the goal of seeing churches established. Though the terms *church planting* and *church-planting movements* are not found in Scripture, the concept of establishing local communities of disciples certainly is. And I am certainly not encouraging the practice of sending inexperienced workers cross-culturally. But I have to wonder whether we have not inadvertently lost sight of the clear, simple and indispensable task entrusted to us by Jesus. We emphasize too often the product (the church) at the expense of the process (disciple-making). We also elevate certain members of the body (professional clergy) to an elite status (church planters) that Christ never intended them to have.

What if a master architect of cathedrals sought to only hire cathedral builders to accomplish his task? The job title certainly has a lofty ring to it. But how many takers would he have? How many stone masons would qualify as cathedral builders? What that architect needs to accomplish his goal is not cathedral builders, but stone masons and carpenters, sculptors and glass workers—skilled tradesmen of all kinds to do what they do best. And even though all the work is accomplished through the workmen, it is the master architect and builder who takes ultimate responsibility for the end product.

So why have we so often put ourselves in the place of the builder, assuming the role of church planter, when Jesus, the Master Architect, commands us to go and *make disciples*, promising that He will be the one to build His church (Matthew 16:18)? Who has what it takes to plant the church? Yes, Paul *planted* and Apollos watered. But they were not referring to the church, but to the gospel seed. And who gave the increase? Who caused that seed to germinate, take root and grow into what ultimately became the church? Paul gives the answer: "I planted, Apollos watered, but *God* was causing the growth" (1 Corinthians 3:6; emphasis added). He adds in verse 9, "For we are God's fellow workers; you are God's field, *God's* building" (emphasis added). The church is not ours to build. God is the One who builds it.

This doesn't mean we simply sow seed, make disciples, and leave them to fend for themselves. Disciples are meant to be gathered in community in the church. The disciple-maker, right from the start, needs to help the new disciple understand the critical importance of life in community. The purpose of spiritual multiplication is always the development of a new community of faith or the growth of an existing one.

The process can be likened to the development of human life. Disciple-making is to church planting what healthy cell multiplication is to the development of a new human being. The fertilized egg multiplies millions of times over, not to produce millions of independent cells, but to form a new body. But here's the thing. The body is formed through healthy cell multiplication. There are no super cells tasked with manufacturing cells and building them into a body. Every cell comes with the built-in capacity to reproduce itself. As it does, the body begins to take shape, individual parts take on their unique roles, and functions begin to emerge.

The responsibility for forming the body does not depend on one single cell, or even two cells. The responsibility is God's. And He forms the body using each and every cell. Certainly God uses gifted men and women to facilitate this process in disciple-making. But they need to be careful not to usurp the role of the Divine Builder and do for the cells what they need to learn to do for themselves—reproduce the life of Jesus in others.

SEVEN SIMPLE WORDS

As I consider the often complex procedures surrounding the call and preparation for today's missionary endeavor, it just seems so much more complicated than the simple seven-word command to "go therefore and make disciples of all nations..." (Matthew 28:19a). The idea that the greatest of Jesus' mandates should be reserved for a select few who spend years just *preparing* for a "missionary call to full-time, church-planting ministry" seems out of sync with two things: what I hear Christ saying and what I see the early disciples doing.

The very notion that there is such a thing as "full-time ministry" is one of the greatest disservices we in the West have done to the body of

---

We have marginalized the vast majority of believers from actively participating in the Great Commission by essentially saying, "You can pray, you can give us your money, and you can even take a short-term trip. But leave the full-time missionary task to us professionals."

Christ. I have heard pastors and missionaries speak countless times of being "called to full-time ministry" as if it were some intermediate step between heaven and earth! We have wrongly communicated to 99 percent of Jesus' followers that there are two classes of Christians—those who are "called to ministry" and everyone else. We have marginalized the vast majority of believers from actively participating in the Great Commission by essentially saying, "You can pray, you can give us your money, and you can even take a short-term trip. But leave the full-time missionary task to us professionals."

I do not question that God gave to the church apostles, prophets, evangelists, pastors and teachers. But why did He give them? He did so "for the equipping of the saints for the work of service..." (Ephesians 4:12a). The King James Version of the Bible uses the phrase, "for the work of the *ministry*..." (emphasis added).[1] Every single believer is called to do ministry! Ministry is not the exclusive domain of the clergy, but the privilege and calling of all believers.

The Protestant Reformation was, among other things, an attempt to recapture the rightful priesthood of all believers from the religious establishment. Luther longed for the day when, in his own words, "we shall recover that joyful liberty in which we shall understand that we are all equal in every right, and shall shake off the yoke of tyranny, and know that he who is a Christian has Christ, and he who has Christ has all things that are Christ's, and can do all things."[2]

A while back I received a note from one of the faithful servants of Christ who has supported mine and Jerusha's work financially for the past six years. It read, "I pray regularly that God would use me in a capacity like yours, and I long for the day when I would be free from what I do now to engage in ministry on a missionary level." Though I admire this man's longing to give himself more fully to the work of ministry, something in me reacts to his statement. It saddens me that we have so successfully convinced believers that "religious professionals" are in ministry and "regular Christians" are not. The fact is, my friend *is* engaged in ministry! He *is* being used to impact the world. In fact, he spends more time rubbing shoulders with unbelievers than I ever will! It was to people such as my friend, not just to the apostles, that Jesus said, "You are the salt of the earth.... You are the light of the world" (Matthew 5:13a, 14a).

In her essay *Why Work?*, British writer Dorothy Sayers rightly observed, "In nothing has the church so lost her hold on reality as in the failure to understand and respect the secular vocation. She has allowed work and religion to become separate departments...."[3] In a similar vein, the authors of *Going Public With Your Faith* wrote, "If you and your pastor go to work for different reasons, then at least one of you is going to work for the wrong reason."[4]

MOBILIZING THE MANY

For centuries, we have primarily mobilized and trained "religious workers" for the harvest. I humbly suggest that there is a better way—mobilizing *all believers* for the harvest.

Is this not what we see in the example of the early church? It was not just the apostles who went into the entire world with the gospel. In fact, in some instances it was just the opposite. When persecution struck the rapidly growing church of Jerusalem, we are told that everyone *except* the apostles scattered throughout Judea and Samaria and "went about preaching the word" (Acts 8:1, 4). When Paul, one of the few "religious professionals" sent out by the church as a missionary, made disciples in the city of Thessalonica, the Thessalonian Christians became such ardent witnesses that Paul later wrote, "For the word of the Lord has sounded forth from you, not only in Macedonia and Achaia, but also in every place your faith toward God has gone forth, so that we have no need to say anything" (1 Thessalonians 1:8).

Where were the apostles fifteen years after the birth of the church? For the most part they were back in Jerusalem while the missionary movement was being carried out by ordinary believers.

Some fifteen years after the birth of the church in Jerusalem, when there arose a controversy about Gentile believers being required to observe the law, a delegation of believers was appointed to go up to Jerusalem, *to the apostles,* to obtain a ruling on this matter. So where were the apostles fifteen years after the birth of the church? Were they spread throughout the world as Great Commission missionaries? No. For the most part they were back in Jerusalem while the missionary movement was being carried out by ordinary believers.

A MODEL WORTH REPEATING

One of the greatest missionary movements in history took place in the eighteenth century when a group of Christians known as the Moravian Brethren sent out thousands of cross-cultural workers, not as professional clergy, but as secular professionals. They used their skills as tradesmen to open doors and support their work as lay missionaries. History tells us that one out of every sixty Moravians lived and worked as a self-supported, cross-cultural minister of the gospel. Today the ratio of cross-cultural workers to the total evangelical population is closer to 1:1,000—few of whom are doing so by means of their secular profession.

Why is it that after two thousand years of missionary activity we have not yet accomplished the task of making disciples of all nations? Why is it that in a world marked by explosive technological advances and the unprecedented connectedness afforded by global communications, travel, economics, immigration and a worldwide thirst for English, there are still so many who have never heard the gospel or had an opportunity to understand or respond to it?

It is certainly not due to any lack in those we have sent or the work they have done. One of the primary reasons is that we have marginalized much of the body of Christ when it comes to their personal involvement in taking the gospel to the nations.

CHAPTER 04

MAKING DISCIPLE-MAKERS

My friend Kyle was recently traveling around Delhi, India. Riding through the streets in one of the thousands of taxis that compete for space in the congested city, he noticed the dashboard was lined with little idols representing some of the more than three hundred thousand gods worshipped in that great land. Curious to understand the driver's religious beliefs, he began to ask him about each of the gods. "That is the one who is supposed to protect me," explained the driver, "and that one there, he is supposed to give me wealth. He is no good at all." After a few minutes of interaction about the man's little collection of gods, Kyle decided to ask the man what he knew about Jesus. "Have you ever heard of Jesus?" Kyle asked. Pausing for a few seconds to reflect, the driver replied, "No, I have never heard of that one."

Imagine that! How is it possible that in the capital city of the world's second most populous nation, there are people like that taxi driver who have never even *heard* of Jesus, much less believed in Him?

Are you aware that there are still nearly 2.5 billion people alive on earth today who have never heard the good news of the gospel? A third of the world has never even *heard* of Jesus! Another two billion, many of them living in post-Christian or Catholic countries, have had some exposure to the Christian faith but have no understanding of the gospel and little opportunity to encounter an authentic follower of Jesus. And it is estimated that by 2025, the world's population will expand by another two billion inhabitants, most of whom will be born in places where the gospel is least known.

Even in a world of trillion-dollar national debts, one billion is still a big number. Consider this: from the moment Jesus rose from the dead until the present day, barely one billion minutes have passed. Yes, minutes. Yet there are currently some two billion people on earth who have never once heard of Jesus. And another two billion are on the way.

What if Jesus had waited until today to launch the church with the 120 followers who had been gathered in the upper room? Would they have been able to reach the world in their lifetime had they been faced with the staggering number of people alive on earth today? If we were to start with 120 fervent followers of Jesus, send them out from one of our megacities and charge each of them with making a gospel presentation to one new person every hour, ten hours a day, 365 days a year, and if they were to keep doing it for the next hundred years, how far would they get? They wouldn't even put a dent in a billion. After one hundred years of non-stop gospel sharing, just over forty-three million people would have heard the gospel once.

Fortunately, Jesus didn't merely tell His original followers to go and share the gospel with all nations. Nor did He tell them to go plant churches among all nations. He told them to do something far more powerful than that. "Therefore go and make disciples of all the nations, baptizing them in the name of the Father and of the Son and of the Holy Spirit, and teaching them to obey everything I have commanded you" (Matthew 28:19–20a, NIV).

Did you catch that? Disciples have to be taught *to obey everything Jesus commanded*, which logically would include the very thing He had just commanded—*to go and make more disciples!* Disciple-making is incumbent on every disciple and every disciple's disciple right down to the present day. Western Christianity has been successful at making converts to fill the church. But there is a better way: making disciple-makers to *be* the church.

So, what if we started doing that?

I have already acknowledged that my son Joel is not a church planter in the classic sense of the word. But could he be a disciple-maker? What if Joel, responding to Jesus' mandate, asked God to give him just one disciple this year? What if through prayer and the witness of his words and life, God should graciously grant him the joy of seeing one of his Chinese co-workers come to faith in Christ and start growing? Then, what if next year as they continued in their discipling relationship, they both began praying that God would give them each one new disciple? And what if that second year God again graciously responded to their faith and obedience and gave each of them one new disciple who began growing in his or her faith? That would make four disciples at various stages of maturity. And what if in the third year, as those four disciples continued in their discipling relationship with each other, they each asked God to give them a new disciple? How long would it take for Joel, his disciples

Disciple-making is incumbent on every disciple and every disciple's disciple right down to the present day.

and his disciples' disciples to thoroughly transform not only that city of seven million people, but the whole country of China?

Before I answer that question, understand clearly that I'm not talking about an entire organization of professional missionaries doing this. I'm talking about starting with one ordinary, passionate follower of Jesus. I'm not talking about fifty thousand full-time Western missionaries doing this. I'm talking about one twenty-five-year-old disciple who has chosen to live and work overseas. I'm not talking about the estimated six hundred million evangelical believers in the world doing this. I'm talking about one. One believer… one disciple… once a year… multiplied year after year.

What would be the impact? Believe it or not, in thirty-three years there would be as many as eight billion disciples of Jesus on earth—in other words, more than the entire population of the world today.

One believer… one disciple… once a year… multiplied year after year.

It might be argued that one disciple per year is too ambitious for a passionate follower of Jesus, given the fact that he works a secular job full time. Maybe he needs two years to make a disciple. Maybe he needs three. But even at that pace, a single disciple-maker would transform the entire world in one long lifetime of ninety-nine years.

How are we doing with our disciple-making mandate? There are roughly fifty thousand vocational missionaries from the West who have responded to Jesus' commission to go to the nations. The majority of them would call themselves church-planting missionaries. But since the Great Commission actually says to *make disciples*, let's call them what Jesus calls them: *disciple-makers*. These vocational ministers of the gospel are essentially *disciple-making specialists*—men and women who have been trained, sent and paid a full-time salary to give themselves fully to making disciples in the nations of the world.

So how are we doing? Well, unless there's something wrong with my math, it would appear that we're not doing so well.

In an article published in the January/February 2011 issue of *Mission Frontiers* magazine, editor Rick Wood states the problem in these terms:

> Our churches in the West seem to be succeeding at lesser things while failing at Jesus' core strategy for world evangelization. We are succeeding in collecting tens of billions of dollars each year to gather large crowds into beautiful and expensive church buildings on Sunday. We have succeeded in putting on a great show and developing programs that attract people to our churches. In the process we have put an unbearable burden on our pastors to do nearly all the ministry while failing to activate the laity. As a result many pastors are skating on the edge of burnout, while the majority of church members do not see that God has any other role for them except as spectators. In short, we are largely failing to develop mature followers of Jesus who are able to make disciples who can make disciples. The people in our churches are not growing to spiritual maturity where they are able to carry on the work of spreading the gospel within our own culture, not to mention cross-culturally to every tribe and tongue. This is having a devastating impact on our ability to bring the gospel to the ends of the earth.
>
> The dirty little secret of missions is that we are sending missionaries all over the world who have not demonstrated the ability to make disciples who can make disciples. Most have not seen or participated in effective models of church-planting or discipleship at home, but we send them out in the hope that going cross-culturally will turn them into effective church planters and disciplers. This is wishful thinking at best.[1]

In his book *Jesus Christ: Disciplemaker*, Bill Hull agrees: "I have not mellowed in my belief that making disciples is indeed the primary and exclusive work of the church. The fact that the church is weaker than ever and shrinking is the evidence that we still haven't got it.... The problem at its root is that we have accepted a non-discipleship Christianity that leads to plenty of motion, activity and conferences but no lasting transformation."[2]

In *The Complete Book of Discipleship*, Hull writes, "We evangelicals accept and even encourage a two-level Christian experience in which only serious Christians pursue and practice discipleship, while grace and forgiveness is enough for everyone else.... I find it both sad and appalling that we've used the great doctrine of justification by faith and God's grace to teach that people don't really need to follow Jesus to be Christians."[3]

Dietrich Bonheoffer rightly observes, "Christianity without discipleship is always Christianity without Christ."[4]

Look at it this way. If I were an insurance salesman yet didn't sell a single insurance policy in an entire year, would you call me an insurance salesman? Of course not. You'd call me unemployed! If I claimed to be a transmission specialist and you came to ask me a few questions about your car's transmission in need of repair, our conversation would go something like this:

"How long have you been in the transmission business?"

"Oh, I've been in it for about three years now."

"Do you mind telling me how many transmissions you repaired last month?"

"I didn't actually repair any last month," I sheepishly admit.

Supposing that it was just a bad month due to the slowdown in the economy, you ask about last year. Again, I admit that I hadn't fixed any transmissions in that time period. To your amazement, you eventually discover that in my three years in business, I haven't actually mended a single transmission. Instead, I've been reading a lot of books on the topic and teaching a course on transmission repair at the local community college.

Would you entrust your transmission to me? Would you call me a specialist? Not in a million years! The fact of the matter is this: if the same standards of productivity and effectiveness that are expected in the business world were applied to Great Commission ministries, some would soon be out of business!

The fact of the matter is this: if the same standards of productivity and effectiveness that are expected in the business world were applied to the Great Commission ministries, some would soon be out of business!

The church in the West has made the Great Commission a mandate for full-time religious professionals—"elite believers" so to speak. But Jesus intended it as a mandate for *all believers*. The church in the West has excelled at making converts who fill the church. But Jesus commanded us to make disciple-makers who will *be* the church. Failure to recognize these important distinctions in Jesus' mandate to the church is at the root of our failure to fully accomplish the task.

So what would it look like if we began doing what Jesus told us to do? What is a disciple? And how do you make one?

CHAPTER 05

LEARNING TO LOVE LIKE JESUS

Peter Ash is a man on a mission. He is out to eradicate the senseless slaughter of "ghosts." His story leaped off the pages of the February 28, 2009, edition of the *National Post* with the headline, "[British Columbia] Man Pledges to End the Slaughter of the Ghosts of Tanzania."[1]

The ghosts of Tanzania are not spirits. They're people—albino African children, to be exact—and they're being slaughtered like animals. Trafficking body parts of these "ghosts" is big business. "A single albino leg," the article explains, "will fetch upwards of $1,000 in a gruesome market controlled by powerful Tanzanian witch doctors who grind the bones into potions and repurpose them as good-luck charms for struggling miners and fishermen."

Ash writes, "Because the belief exists that the albino is a ghost or an omen or a curse, the newborn is sometimes taken out back by the midwife where she suffocates it or breaks its neck, and then tells the father that the child was stillborn. Those who survive past infancy with a full set of arms, legs, hair, genitals, and blood are worth up to $30,000, the equivalent of four decades of wages in that country."

Albino body parts are usually hacked off while the victim is still alive. Viviana was one such victim. In the middle of the night, a gang of men charged into her room, hauled her outside, and pinned her to the ground. They hacked off one of her legs and escaped into the darkness while her sister screamed in horror. Viviana was actually one of the lucky ones. She only lost one leg and even survived the attack. "In some cases," explains Ash, "the attackers slit the throat first and drain the blood into a pot. One mom told how they came in and slit the girl's throat, and drank the blood on the spot." Somewhere between fifty and one hundred albino children in Tanzania have lost their lives. Others have been maimed for life and continue to live with the threat of further dismemberment.

When he first learned of the albinos' plight, Ash, a Caucasian albino, knew he had to do something to help. So he launched Under the Same Sun—an organization committed to exposing the atrocities and pressuring the Tanzanian government to take action against the brutal injustice.

As I read the story of this man's crusade against evil, I wondered what it was about this man and his mission that riveted the attention of so many. After all, there are millions of people all over the world who are oppressed, abused, starving and worse. Millions have lost their lives in genocides, and the world has hardly noticed. So why would the story of a few hundred albino children arrest anyone's attention?

I believe the answer lies in the power of impacting one person's life. Making a profound difference in one specific child's life is more powerful than describing the plight of a million anonymous people. As callous as it may sound, Josef Stalin was right about human nature when he said, "A single death is a tragedy. A million deaths is a statistic."[2] Peter Ash is focused on the few. He has a focused passion to make a real difference in a few lives. I don't know whether he is a follower of Jesus, but I do know this: he understands that changing the world begins with changing one life.

IMPACT HAPPENS CLOSE UP

When it comes to the task of disciple-making, the same principle stands true: the world is not transformed by making a superficial difference in many lives, but by making a profound difference in a few. Real, lasting life-change takes place not at the macro-level, but at the micro-level, one on one, close up. I will always remember what my seminary professor Howard Hendricks said about deep impact: "You can impress people from a distance, but you can only impact them close up." You change the world by changing a life. And you change a life by making a disciple. It's what Jesus did. He could have impressed us from the heavens, but He chose to impact us by entering our world and pouring His life into a few men who, in turn, did the same.

In the West, the church has flourished when it comes to *impressing people from a distance* but has failed when it comes to *impacting them close up.* We have championed the way of impressing the many, but have often missed the better way of impacting the few. The disciple-making mandate is all about impacting the few.

This is not just the mandate of mission organizations—it is the mandate of all believers. Author Robert Coleman notes in his book *The Master Plan of Discipleship*, "If making disciples of all nations is not the heartbeat of our life, something is wrong, either with our understanding of Christ's church or our willingness to walk in His way."[3]

WHAT IS A DISCIPLE?

In order to understand our disciple-making mandate, we need to understand what a disciple is. The problem is that the word *disciple* has been so commonly used and applied in a certain way that we think we know what it means when we really don't.

The word *discipleship* is a case in point. Try initiating a conversation with some fellow believers about discipleship and I can almost guarantee that if they have any interest in the subject, one of the first questions they'll ask you will be, "What material do you use?"

Why do we tend to ask about curriculum and books? Because here in the West, discipleship has become almost synonymous with a curriculum or program. People wrongly believe that if you have gone through a certain series of studies on the Christian life you have been "discipled."

In the West, the church has flourished when it comes to *impressing people from a distance*, but has failed when it comes to *impacting them close up*.

Our first challenge is to understand the word as it was used in Scripture rather than how it has been used in our Western culture.

What does the word *disciple* really mean? The most commonly used synonym would be *follower*. In the New Testament, the word *disciple* is used to refer not only to fully formed followers, but to "pre-faith" followers. In John 6 it was clearly used to denote a group of followers who were not yet believers. Describing this group of followers who had been offended by Jesus' teaching, John writes, "As a result of this many of His *disciples* withdrew and were not walking with Him anymore" (John 6:66; emphasis added). Were these believers who had lost their salvation? No. They were seekers, new pre-faith followers who quit following Him short of placing their trust in Him.

On the other end of the spectrum, the term *disciple* described a mature, Christ-like follower. This is certainly the most common New Testament usage of the word. We are told in Acts 11:26 that the followers of Jesus looked so much like Him that "the disciples were first called Christians in Antioch." A brand new term was coined for Jesus-followers. These followers, unlike the ones in John 6, looked so much like Jesus that they were called *Christians,* meaning "little Christs."

Our ministry to people prior to their conversion is a process and not simply an "evangelistic event."

So if a disciple is a follower at any stage of following, then the work of disciple-making actually begins *before* conversion. Traditionally, most have referred to this pre-conversion ministry as evangelism, while only the post-conversion period is seen as discipleship. I would like to suggest, however, that if the word *disciple* can be used of an unbeliever, as in John 6, then it follows that disciple-making takes place anywhere along the continuum.

Is this simply a question of semantics? In one sense, yes. But what we learn from John 6 is that our ministry to people prior to their conversion is a process and not simply an "evangelistic event." Unfortunately, however, evangelism has too often been seen as just that—an event where the goal is to give people a gospel presentation and call for a decision, regardless of where they might be in their understanding of, or interest in, Jesus. The result of such indiscriminate "evangelism" can be more hurtful than it is helpful. Lewis Sperry Chafer, founder of Dallas Theological Seminary and passionate evangelist, wrote this:

> The examples of soulwinning in the New Testament present a conspicuous contrast to some examples of presentday evangelism. So far as the divine record shows, there seemed to be little urging or coaxing, nor was any person dealt with individually who had not first

> given evidence of a divinely wrought sense of need. It is recorded that Peter directed the converts at Pentecost in the way of life after they were "pricked in their heart, and said unto Peter and to the rest of the apostles, Men and brethren, what shall we do?" So also there is no record that Paul and Silas pleaded with the Philippian jailor to become a Christian before he had any such desire; but rather, after a great change had taken place in his whole attitude which compelled him to fall tremblingly before them and say, "Sirs, what must I do to be saved?" did they personally direct him to "believe on the Lord Jesus Christ." Peter does not send for Cornelius—Cornelius reaches out for Peter. And Saul is led into the light almost without human aid or direction. In view of this allimportant divine preparation for salvation, it is clear that all evangelism...which does not wait for the movings of the Spirit in the hearts of the unsaved is [thus] removed from true cooperation with God, and is in danger of hindering souls.[4]

A less dichotomized view of the process of people coming to faith and maturity in Christ is to see disciple-making as the life-long process of helping people move toward Jesus—toward *faith* in Jesus and toward *fullness* in Jesus. The moment of conversion is simply the fulcrum of the disciple-making process. A very important fulcrum. It's the threshold of passing from darkness to light, from death to life, from hell to heaven. But it is not the finish line, nor is it the starting point of the disciple-making process.

Consequently, when I pray for God to provide me with people to disciple, I ask Him for disciples on both sides of the cross—those who are moving from unbelief to *faith*, and those who are moving from initial faith to *fullness* of maturity.

A LEARNING PROCESS

While the most common understanding of the word *disciple* is *follower,* the most accurate definition in terms of what the Greek word actually means is *learner.* A disciple is a learner, an apprentice, someone who is learning to imitate his master. I like the word *learner* for the simple reason that it conveys the truth that it is a *process*. I have not fully learned to be like my Master, but I am learning. I am a learner. I am in process and that process will continue as long as I live.

Jesus defines a disciple in very clear terms, saying that His disciples will be distinguished by three primary marks or characteristics.

Learning to Love Like Jesus

Most of us would have no trouble agreeing on the first one. *Love*. Not knowledge. Not a conversion experience. Not church membership. Not spiritual gifts. Not doctrinal purity. But *love*. "By this all men will know that you are *My* disciples," said Jesus, "if you have love for one another" (John 13:35; emphasis added). As if that wasn't clear enough, He repeats Himself a few verses later in John 15:9. "Just as the Father has loved Me, I have also loved you; abide in My love." And again in verse 12: "This is My commandment, that you love one another, just as I have loved you." And yet again in verse 17: "This I command you, that you love one another, just as I have loved you."

Authentic followers of Jesus are those who *love*. They love God, they love one another, and they love people. These followers express that love through their unique gifting and personality, but they love nonetheless.

One of the most effective disciple-makers I know just happens to be one of the most loving people I know. His name is Chris. When you are with Chris, you feel as though you are the most important person in the world. He may have a calendar filled to overflowing, but Chris will make you feel like you are the top priority on his agenda. He genuinely loves people and demonstrates it by the time he spends pouring his life into theirs. One of the young Brazilians in whom Chris had deeply invested commented, "Chris is not like other missionaries. He has time for people." Though he didn't mean it as an indictment of other foreign workers, it certainly spoke volumes. Followers of Jesus learn to love like Jesus.

Learning to Lose Like Jesus

The second distinguishing mark of a disciple, according to Jesus, is really the first mark carried to its fullest expression. In John 15:12–13 Jesus said, "This is My commandment that you *love* one another, just as I have loved you. Greater love has no one than this, that one *lay down his life* for his friends" (emphasis added). *That* is sacrifice.

Five other times Jesus defined His followers in terms of sacrifice or self-denial (Matthew 10:38; Mark 8:34; Luke 9:23, 14:27). And Matthew 16:24 says, "If anyone wishes to come after Me, he must deny himself, and take up his cross and follow Me." Four of those times Jesus adds words similar to these: "For whoever wishes to save his life will lose it; but whoever loses his life for My sake, he is the one who will save it."

To follow Jesus is to lose one's life. This might mean losing one's family, friends, wealth, financial security, reputation or whatever it takes to bring glory to God and the gospel. It is to lose life in order to discover life. In Luke 14:27, Jesus was very clear about what a *disciple* is. "Whoever does not carry his own cross and come after Me *cannot be My disciple*" (emphasis added).

Interestingly, love and sacrifice were the two characteristics that Paul used to describe his ministry with the Thessalonian believers who were so fruitful. Paul writes, "In every place your faith toward God has gone forth, so that we had no need to say anything" (1 Thessalonians 1:8).

How did Paul succeed in making such disciples? Listen to what he says: "But we proved to be gentle among you, as a nursing mother tenderly cares for her own children." Now that's love! He continues, "Having so fond an affection for you, we were well-pleased to impart to you not only the gospel of God but also our *own lives*..." (1 Thessalonians 2:7–8; emphasis added). And that's sacrifice! How did Paul succeed in all he did? Through love and sacrifice.

In the first two verses of Ephesians 5, Paul talks again about love and sacrifice. He writes, "Therefore be imitators of God...." I am supposed to imitate God? How does anyone imitate God? What does that look like? Paul explains. "Walk in *love*, just as Christ also loved you and *gave Himself up* for us, an offering and a *sacrifice* to God as a fragrant aroma" (emphasis added). Imitating God means walking in sacrificial love for God and people. Love and sacrifice.

To recap, a disciple is marked by *love*. He loves God and people. A disciple is also marked by *sacrifice*—laying down his life and dying to self.

Learning to Live Like Jesus

What is the third mark of a disciple according to Jesus? The Great Commission of Matthew 28:19–20 is clear. "Go therefore and make disciples of all nations...teaching them to *observe all* that I commanded you..." (emphasis added). Disciples are recognized by *obedience* to all that Jesus commanded. This would include, first and foremost, what He had commanded them right here—to go and make disciples who, in turn, go and make disciples.

Jesus puts it all together for us in John 15:12–14 where He says, "This is My commandment, that you *love* one another.... Greater love has no one than this, that one *lay down his life* for his friends. You are My friends if you *do* what I *command* you" (emphasis added). In three short verses

Jesus captures the essence of what it means to be His disciple. It entails three things: love, obedience and self-sacrifice (LOSS). Disciples are distinguished by LOSS.

Here is how we at Crossworld have defined *disciple*: a disciple is one who is learning to live and love like Jesus and helps others to do the same.

All three characteristics of a disciple are captured in the single word: *love*. Jesus said that to love is to lay down your life, and that if you love Him, you will obey His commandments. *Love* involves *obedience* and *sacrifice*. The key, therefore, to achieving the Great Commission is to obey the Great Commandments. The way you make a disciple is by loving God supremely and loving people sacrificially.

Here is how we at Crossworld have defined *disciple*: a disciple is one who is learning to live and love like Jesus and helps others to do the same.

First, the disciple is *learning* because a disciple is, by definition, a learner.

Second, the disciple is learning two primary things: to live like Jesus (in *obedience* to God) and to *love* like Jesus (in *sacrifice* for people).

Third, the disciple is *helping others to do the same*—in other words, he is committed to reproducing. Discipleship is not just about me becoming like Jesus. It's about reproducing Jesus in another person's life.

The disciple-making mandate is not about mere conversion. It is not even about transformation. The disciple-making mandate is about reproduction. Until we reproduce, we have not yet done what Jesus asked us to do.

CHAPTER / 06

THREE INDISPENSABLE INGREDIENTS OF DISCIPLE-MAKING

How does a disciple who is learning to live and love like Jesus help others to do the same? How does a disciple make a disciple who, in turn, will make a disciple? What does the disciple-making process look like?

Before answering these questions, let me say this: if the answers are not simple, disciple-making will never be reproducible. If your disciple cannot take what you have imparted to him and do it in someone else's life, it is not biblical disciple-making. Your disciple has not learned to obey the very heart of Jesus' disciple-making mandate.

The apostle Paul, in 2 Timothy 2:2, speaks of disciple-making to the fourth generation—what some have called *God's 4G Network*. He says, "The things which you have heard from me in the presence of many witnesses, entrust these to faithful men who will be able to teach others also." What that means is a disciple-maker cannot be satisfied with the conversion or even transformation of a single disciple. He needs to strive to impart to his disciple the "DNA" of spiritual reproduction. The goal of a disciple-maker is not merely making another disciple, but rather *making another disciple-maker.* For that multi-generational reproductive process to happen over and over again, it better be simple.

> **The goal of a disciple-maker is not merely making another disciple, but rather *making another disciple-maker.***

Neither Jesus nor His disciples wrote a discipleship manual, other than the Bible, to describe the process because it is simple. Not easy, but simple. Both loving God's Word supremely by obeying whatever He commands and loving people sacrificially to the point of even laying down your life are certainly not easy, but they're not complicated either.

Let me tell you how we at Crossworld have defined disciple-making. Then I'll explain how we arrived at that conclusion. Disciple-making is helping people everywhere to live and love like Jesus by imparting God's truth through authentic relationships wherever life happens.

To put it even more simply, disciple-making is all about three things: truth, relationship and life.

1 // LOVING TRUTH

Disciple-making is all about truth—*God's truth*, to be exact. It means loving God and His Word supremely. It is not about a discipleship curriculum. It's about embracing a love letter from God. It's about being so hungry for God that you pour His Word—His love letter to you—into your heart and then back out of your life into another person.

Five of the most powerful words ever spoken to me by another human being were spoken by the man who was to one day become my father-in-law. Pastor Jerry, as he was fondly called, was a no-nonsense youth pastor in San Diego who was known for his passionate love for the Word of God. When I met his daughter during my final year of college, I had no idea what I was getting into. One day, about eight months into my relationship with Jerusha and after I had already asked for his daughter's hand in marriage, I went to lunch with Pastor Jerry. Wanting to impress him with my commitment to spiritual growth, I decided to ask him a really "profound" question.

As he sat there across the table from me, I asked, "Pastor Jerry, do you see anything in my life that I need to work on?" I have no idea what I was hoping for in an answer. Perhaps I was imagining that he'd just affirm my amazing spiritual depth for such a young man and encourage me on my merry (naïve) way. But that is certainly not what I got. Without taking a breath between my question and his answer, he just looked me straight in the eye and replied, "You don't love God's Word."

I sat in shock for a moment. I wanted to argue with him. *What do you mean I don't love God's Word? I almost never miss a day of personal devotions. I am currently memorizing four new verses every week. I just graduated from a Christian college and am starting a pastoral position next week. What do you mean I don't love God's Word?*

But, in my heart of hearts, I knew he was right.

Apart from the Word of God, Pastor Jerry's five simple words and the change process that they initiated have made more of an impact in my life than any other factor. Western discipleship methods have tended toward a programmed, pedagogical transmission of truth. Jesus' way, the better way, calls for us to passionately embrace the truth.

Perhaps the greatest deficiency in our Western disciple-making methods is that we try to impart something we don't have. If God's Word is not filling my heart and being lived out in my life, I have nothing to give my disciple. No curriculum, no matter how good it is, can ever replace a personal and fervent love for God's Word. God's truth is the *content* for making a disciple.

2 // LOVING PEOPLE

Loving relationships are the *context* for making disciples. Disciples are made by imparting God's truth through *authentic relationships*. When truth is communicated devoid of relationship, it is often rejected—especially if the truth being shared is not what the person wants to hear. It's not that relationship is a prerequisite for imparting truth. God's truth is well able to transform hearts in and of itself. But a loving relationship is a catalyst that enhances the transmission of truth.

Living life in relationship with other believers or neighbors is rapidly becoming a thing of the past. We are a relationally challenged society. Compared with much of the world, North American relationships are rather superficial. Our values of time, efficiency and independence reduce relationships to a minimum. "How's it going?" is not a question but a mere greeting. There is much truth in the words of my African friend who said, speaking of Westerners, "You have watches, but we have time." Even in the church, many believers have relationships that go no deeper than a handshake on Sunday morning and maybe an additional one-hour small group study for the highly engaged.

Truth without love is dead orthodoxy—or as Paul put it, no better than a "noisy gong or a clanging cymbal" (1 Corinthians 13:1). Truth without relationship is sterile. Remember that the apostle Paul described his disciple-making ministry as imparting "not only the gospel of God but also our *own lives*..." (1 Thessalonians 2:8; emphasis added). It is precisely what God did when "...the Word became flesh, and dwelt among us..." (John 1:14).

Apologist and youth expert Josh McDowell has written and spoken broadly on the glaring failure of North American evangelicalism to successfully transmit the faith to the next generation. To what does he attribute this failure? Truth without relationship. When describing the futility of trying to impart one's faith apart from meaningful relationship, he said, "Rules without relationship leads to… rebellion."[1]

Truth is most effectively transmitted through relationship.

Parents who lack a vibrant faith in God and a loving relationship with their children are far more likely to see their children defect from the faith. Obviously, it's not always the fault of the parent. The young person's sinful heart and free will are certainly primary factors. Indeed, Adam and Eve had a perfect Father and lived in a perfect world, yet they chose to walk away. Nonetheless, the vital importance of cultivating one's relationship with God and His children cannot not be ignored. Truth is most effectively transmitted through relationship.

Western discipleship has tended to be highly *transactional.* In other words, "I, the teacher, have truth. You, the disciple, need it. I will transmit it to you in a transaction that will take place on Tuesday evening at 7 p.m." Certainly this is not true of all discipleship ministries, but it has been true of many in the West. Jesus modeled a better way for us: *relational disciple-making.*

3 // LIVING LIFE

The third critical component of effective disciple-making is life itself—doing it *where life happens.* God is a relational God who imparted truth in the context of life—to shepherds in fields, to fishermen in boats, and to disillusioned followers as they walked along a dusty road. Is it possible that in our transmission of God's living truth, we have come to rely too heavily on the artificial atmosphere of a program or an institution? Pastors are trained in seminaries, believers are trained in discipleship programs, and children are trained in Sunday school classes or youth groups. I am not saying that there is no place for such training environments. I am simply suggesting that classrooms and curriculums are poor substitutes for real-life relationships. Truth is best learned in the crucible of life.

My father was a pastor who modeled what he taught. What I heard on Sunday morning was what I saw Monday through Saturday. He was certainly not perfect, but his ability to live truth made a powerful impact on me as well as on many others. A number of years ago, I crossed paths with someone who had known my father when he was a young pastor in the country church where this man had attended as a teenager.

Though some thirty-five years had elapsed since that time, his recollection of my father was quite sharp. "Do you want to know my first memory of your dad? My father was a farmer and was down in a hole that he was digging when your dad drove in to pay him a visit, wearing a suit and tie. But rather than waiting for my dad to climb out of the hole, your dad whipped off his coat and tie, grabbed a shovel, jumped down in the hole and started digging." That simple act communicated truth to that teenage boy and his father in a way that no sermon or Sunday school lesson ever could.

I am not saying that modeling the truth is a substitute for speaking it. I am saying that truth is best taught when it is *also modeled.* Today's younger generation loves to *hang out.* Many of them have a strong aversion to anything programmed or planned. But though disciple-making is not about programs, neither is it just about "hanging" in a coffee shop. Real disciple-making is a dynamic, passionate pursuit of God's truth with another person. When this happens in the context of a loving relationship where truth is modeled in real life, the result is powerful, lasting transformation.

INCARNATIONAL MINISTRY IS NOTHING NEW

Jesus' coming to earth as a man is what we call the *incarnation.* That word is the same one from which we get words like *carnivore* or *chili con carne.* A carnivore is an animal that eats *meat. Chili con carne* is chili with *meat* in it. The incarnation was simply the act of God clothing Himself with *meat*—that is, human flesh. To put it another way, it was God removing His divine coat and tie and jumping down into our hole to dig dirt with us, rather than expecting us to climb out of our hole and clean ourselves up to meet with Him. Jesus was the ultimate example of what it means to impart truth through relationship in the context of life.

But long before Jesus did it, God had already communicated to His people, the Hebrew nation, that this was also the way for them to impart His truth from generation to generation. Deuteronomy 6 is referred to by the Jewish people as the *shema*, so called because the word *shema* is the opening word of the passage that begins in verse 4. It reads as follows: "Hear O Israel! The LORD our God, the LORD is one! You shall love the LORD your God with all your heart and with all your soul and with all your might. These words, which I am commanding you today, shall be on your heart. You shall teach them diligently to your sons and shall talk of them when you sit in your house and when you walk by the way and when you lie down and when you rise up" (Deuteronomy 6:4–7).

How did God intend for the Hebrew faith to be passed on? Notice the three crucial elements of imparting truth: *truth, relationship* and *life.* The first one is *truth*: you love God fervently and fill your heart with His truth. Note that before His truth is on your lips, it needs to be in your heart.

Before you can pour it into someone else, you need to pour it into yourself. Perhaps the failure in much of what has been called discipleship is that it is a transmission of truth from the head rather than from the heart.

The second crucial element of imparting truth is a *loving relationship.* For the Hebrew nation, it was the loving relationship of a parent with a child ("teach them diligently to your sons..."). Interestingly, this is the same imagery that Paul used to describe his relationship with his disciples in Thessalonica. The primary context for the propagation of the Hebrew faith was not the synagogue or temple, but the family.

The third critical element in the process of truth transmission is doing it *in the context of life,* or as we have put it in Crossworld's definition of disciple-making, *wherever life happens.* Notice how Jewish parents were told to impart God's truth to their children: "Talk of them when you sit in your house and when you walk by the way and when you lie down and

---

***Truth, relationship* and *life* are an incredibly powerful trio. Anyone who loves God's Word supremely, loves people sacrificially, and shares life incarnationally will impact this world eternally.**

---

when you rise up." In other words, wherever life happened. This could be at the dinner table, in the coffee shop, on the soccer field or during the morning commute to work or school—literally wherever and whenever.

The power of truth spoken at the appropriate moment and reinforced by example is inestimable. I have read some good books on healthy marriage relationships, but most of what I have learned about loving my wife did not come from books. I learned it through God's truth spoken and modeled by my father. Not once do I remember my dad treating my mom with anything but love and respect. If I had ever shown a lack of respect for my mother, the power of my dad's corrective instruction, backed by his example, were plenty to bring me quickly into line.

Today, if I know anything about loving my wife as Christ loved the church, I owe it to my dad who transmitted that truth through a loving relationship right in the home where I grew up.

Truth, relationship and *life* are an incredibly powerful trio. Anyone who loves God's Word supremely, loves people sacrificially, and shares life incarnationally will impact this world eternally.

SEVEN ESSENTIAL ELEMENTS

In summary, let me draw your attention to seven essential elements of Crossworld's disciple-making vision and then share a word of personal application. Remember that we have defined the disciple-making process as helping people everywhere to live and love like Jesus by imparting God's truth through authentic relationships wherever life happens.

1. The *mark* of a disciple is that he is *one who lives and loves like Jesus* in three specific ways: love, obedience and self-sacrifice (LOSS).

2. The *task* of a disciple is to *help others to live and love like Jesus.* In other words, he is committed to spiritual reproduction.

3. The *content* a disciple-maker needs is simply *God's truth.* Read it. Study it. Memorize it. Love it. Pour it into yourself, and then pour it back out into someone else.

4. The *context* necessary for making a disciple is that of *authentic relationships.* A disciple-maker loves people.

5. The *classroom* for making disciples is *life.* Imparting God's truth where people live.

6. The *process* for making a disciple is simply the combination of those three elements: *truth, relationship* and *life.* Disciples are made when God's

truth is imparted through authentic relationships in the classroom of life.

7. And the *scope* of disciple-making is *everywhere*—the whole world. In other words, a disciple develops a global vision.

GOD'S WORD IS ENOUGH

A couple of years ago as I was beginning to wrestle with the meaning and implications of authentic disciple-making for my own life and for the Crossworld family, I was reading one of author Neil Cole's books on disciple-making called *Search and Rescue.* The book is a very practical explanation of the process of life transformation in others. Foundational to his approach is what he calls a *Life Transformation Group* (LTG)—a group of two to four disciples who commit to share life together and encourage one another in three pursuits: God's truth, personal holiness and lost souls.

At the time, I had been struggling with the commonly asked question about a discipleship curriculum. Being very task- and program-oriented, I wanted a framework on which to build my disciple-making plan. How could I just tell people to read the Word and apply it? What kind of discipleship program is that? Yet that was exactly what Cole seemed to be proposing.

I began to think of my own spiritual development and what I would point to as the primary factors in my own growth as a disciple. I had been raised in a pastor's family. I had a four-year Bible college degree and a four-year master's degree from one of the best seminaries in the world. I had been raised on a diet of some of the finest biblical teaching on earth. And yet, as I thought about all those advantages, I realized that the single most transformational factor in my life was my daily practice of personally feeding on the Word of God and applying it to my life.

I decided to ask Jerusha what she thought was the key factor in her spiritual development. And without a moment's hesitation, she replied, "My personal daily study of the Word of God."

It took that convergence of thoughts and facts to illuminate my understanding and ignite my heart with a conviction that if God's Word was sufficient for my own spiritual development, it should also be sufficient for anyone else's spiritual development. I decided that, from that time on, I would not spend hours of time developing studies to spoon-feed future disciples in my life. Instead, I would get them to feed themselves right from the start by reading and obeying God's Word.

At the time, I had recently begun leading a life transformation group with four young men who had asked me to be their spiritual mentor. I immediately decided to change the curriculum to a straight diet of personal Bible reading. We committed to reading between fifteen and twenty-five chapters of Scripture each week. Before I made the switch, I wondered how they would respond. How would a firefighter, an insurance broker, a cabinetmaker and a graphic designer respond to such a challenge?

To my delight, they not only rose to the occasion, they relished it! I still remember what one of them said about a month into the experience. He was a guy who put in long hours at his job and would drive nearly one hundred miles round trip to meet with us. One evening, just as we were about to part ways, he said, "Every time I head home from being together with you guys, I feel like a kid with candy, riding the bus on his way home from a week at summer camp." I sat there listening and thinking to myself, "You've got to be kidding! You work all day, drive one hundred miles, and you feel that good about it?" The pursuit of God's truth, of holiness and of lost people was having a powerful impact on this man. Today, though a thousand miles separate them from me, those men continue to meet to pursue God, holiness and lost people.

Since that day back in 2009, I have been like Peter Ash—a man on a mission to make a difference in a few lives. No longer do I want to be the guy who merely impresses people from a distance with a powerful sermon or a riveting article. I want to impact people close up, a few at a time, by making disciples who make disciples. I am convinced that this is the better way, indeed the only way, to accomplish Christ's commission. This way is accessible to every believer—especially people like my son Joel. And it is for people like him that I have a dream.

by JOHN BERGER, Crossworld's Vice President for Global Operations and Strategy

CHAPTER 07

THE ELUSIVE QUEST FOR LIFE

In *Phenomenon*, a 1996 movie starring John Travolta, the main character George Malley is an amiable auto mechanic whose life takes an astonishing turn. Upon seeing a bright flash of light, he gains instant mental capacities far surpassing any run-of-the-mill genius.

George begins to generate creative ideas on the basis of intuitive scientific understanding. He experiments with methods to improve crop production. He breaks an Air Force code and plays with the government by sending them messages that someone is listening. He develops a prototype for producing photosynthetic energy from normal light bulbs. He even learns Portuguese from reading a book in the passenger seat of a truck during a twenty-minute ride!

But beyond his raw intellectual capacity, George experiences an intense, discerning connection to his environment that allows him to understand and react to the world in abnormal ways. He can feel the "atmospheric energy" telling him an earthquake will take place in just a few days. He can perform mind-over-matter telekinetic feats such as picking up a paper clip that is out of his reach or smashing a mirror across the room.

As word gets out about his superhuman capacities, government officials and university researchers come to him. They want to understand his capabilities and how they could be harnessed for the benefit of mankind.

One day when George falls unconscious, doctors finally discover the unexpected secret behind his amazing transformation: an astrocytoma brain tumor. Tentacles from the tumor extend throughout his brain like connecting threads. The tumor stimulates his brain in such a way that George is able to use more of the brain's previously untapped potential than ever known possible.

As I watched *Phenomenon's* plot unfold, I was struck by how well George Malley's experience reflected the human condition. There is a sad gap between human potential and human reality; what we actually accomplish in life is a poor substitute for what we should be able to accomplish. There has to be more. We know it intuitively.

I believe that this innate sense that the world is not the way it's supposed to be—that if we could just get it right, life would be so much better—is rooted in the fact that creation reflects God's heart. God intended an amazing experience for man. But what we're living is a far cry from that design.

LIFE IN A BROKEN WORLD

Far more than a simple belief that there's a better way to do missions in a changing world, the message of this book is rooted in the conviction that *there's a better way to do life in a broken world.* God designed us for so much more than the ruined existence that humanity experiences. Human beings were created with unfathomable potential to experience life. But there has been a disconnect.

It is for this very reason that Jesus gave to those who would follow Him that great, incarnational, disciple-making mandate. The goal of disciple-making is not merely higher numbers of disciples—after all, even the Pharisees were into making disciples. Nor is the goal merely one of getting people from earth to heaven. The better way—Jesus' way—is all about experiencing soul-satisfying, earth-revolutionizing *life* right now! When we say that we dream of *disciple-makers from all professions bringing God's love to life*, we are not merely talking about the *process*, we're talking about the *product*—thirst-quenching life!

Far more than a simple belief that there's a better way to do missions in a changing world, the message of this book is rooted in the conviction that *there's a better way to do life in a broken world.*

So what exactly is this better way to live? What was the life that we were created for? Why is there such a gap between what could be and what is? And what did Jesus mean when He offered "abundant life"?

WHAT WAS GOD THINKING?

Have you ever wondered why God made you? Or for that matter, why He made anything at all? Those of us who have attended church for many years may be quick to respond with learned truisms such as, "God made us for His pleasure" or "God created everything for His glory." And I agree with these statements. But what do they actually mean?

Let's look for the answer starting back in eternity past.

Before God made the world, did anything exist? Nothing did apart from God. He alone is eternal in the sense of having no beginning. He is the one and only uncaused cause. In other words, before anything or anyone else existed, God was. And He was alone.

If He was alone, was He lonely? No. That's the beauty and mystery of the Trinity. Though God was alone, He was always "with." Throughout eternity past,* the triune Godhead experienced perfectly satisfying love, kindness, friendship and intimacy in and of Himself.

Was He lacking anything? No. Was He unhappy? No. Did He need something or someone to complete Him? No. He was perfectly content and satisfied, full of expressed goodness, joy, love, wisdom and every other delightful attribute we could use to describe Him.

So why did God choose to create if He was fully content within Himself? The simple answer is, to glorify Himself.

God's glory can be understood as the weighty sum total of His marvelous qualities. To glorify God is to sense, admire and proclaim the wonder of those qualities, whether to oneself, to God or to others. And when God glorifies Himself, He reveals those qualities for others to admire. As the crafters of the Westminster Confession of Faith wrote, "It pleased God the Father, Son, and Holy Ghost, *for the manifestation of the glory* of His eternal power, wisdom, and goodness, in the beginning, to create, or make of nothing, the world" (emphasis added).[1]

So who is the beneficiary of God's self-glorification? The very ones who have the pleasure of admiring and thoroughly enjoying God's inde-

---

* If God alone has no beginning, then it seems only logical to conclude that He was alone "forever" in the past; i.e., alone for an infinitely long period of time. Of course, that logic is merely human, as is the assumption that time was somehow relevant prior to God's first act of creation. I am certain that my perception of eternity past as an infinitely long period of time must be flawed. Just another reason to sit awestruck in contemplation of the Eternal One.

scribable beauty. In other words, people.

Stop a minute to consider the pleasure you derive when you experience good things: good food, good art, good music, good friends, good humor, good sex, good entertainment, good architecture, good literature, good golf and good rest. These pleasures are merely a taste of the pleasure God designed for us. Imagine, then, the unparalleled pleasure we can enjoy when we experience the very Source, Creator and Definition of all that is truly good. The kindest, most generous thing God can do for us is to glorify Himself!

While we need to be careful to avoid sliding into man-centered heresy, we need to recognize how much God values our pleasure. In fact, apart from grasping how much joy and delight God intended for us, we do not understand just how good the good news really is.

In a wonderful twist of harmony, God is also the beneficiary, if you will, of His own self-glorification. Not because He longs for our approval or flattery in order to feel better about Himself, but because He experiences joy in expressing His generous love. You might say that God takes great pleasure in giving us pleasure. That is truly good news for us!

When God created, He was thinking of us.* His purpose was to create friends and loyal subjects who would find complete joy, contentment, satisfaction, pleasure and meaning in Him. He chose to bring us into existence to generously, graciously and lovingly pleasure us with Himself. In other words, He gave us *life*.

---

* To ask and answer, "What was God thinking?" is somewhat foolish and requires oversimplification. I am certain that God's thinking and motives in creation must have been much more complex (unfathomable for you and me) than I suggest in the simple text of the chapter. So I am not suggesting that God was thinking exclusively of us. I don't pretend to understand how God intertwines diverse interests and nuances regarding His own supremacy as creation's object of worship, His exaltation of the Son, His polemic against rebels, etc. But I do believe that God's generous love toward us and for our benefit is an essential element of the gospel that is demonstrated in creation.

THE MEANING OF LIFE

God created us for life.

This sounds so obvious...almost silly, unless we understand that life is so much more than simple (and perhaps painful or boring) existence. God did not create us to simply experience a heartbeat, brainwaves, eating, sleeping, growing up, working, retiring and dying. He created us for joy. He made us to be thrilled with His beauty and His creative prowess. He designed us to marvel at His perfections, to enter into the experience of His delightful and awesome qualities and to revel in His love and the depth of His goodness. He created us for life.

When I began to read the Bible with a new sense of what *life* means, I began discovering previously hidden treasures. This good news, I began to realize, is better than I had ever thought.

God did not create us to simply experience a heartbeat, brainwaves, eating, sleeping, growing up, working, retiring and dying. He created us for joy.

In Genesis 1 and 2 we read that creation was good. Not just good, but very good. The man and the woman in the garden had it all: wonderful friendship with their Creator, a beautiful environment at their disposal, and an untarnished intimate relationship with each other. They lived in health, peace, abundance, creativity, meaningful work and joy. What more could they want?

The life God conceived for us was pure delight. Can you imagine the Eternal One strolling through your garden in the cool of the day, calling you to join Him? What a life!

Is that what we see in our world today? Not at all! The world is broken. Death dominates through poverty, pain, conflict, corruption, disease and a litany of evil perversions and limitations of God's design. Creation is groaning, longing to be freed from its rotting degradation.

The reality of death's dominance came alive to me during the nearly seventeen years I taught at the *Séminaire de Théologie Evangélique de Port-au-Prince* in Haiti. I had examined the great truths of the Bible in the comfort of the Dallas Theological Seminary library. But in Haiti, I was teaching students who would, in turn, teach others who faced life conditions that most Americans only vaguely hear about. Haiti's troubles are legendary: grinding poverty, disease, violent corruption, spiritism, immorality, distrust, pollution, kidnapping and despair. While there is much beauty and joy worth celebrating in Haiti, that society is mostly known for decay and suffering.

Haiti's pain has a face. Henri befriended me soon after I moved to Haiti. He lived with his wife and daughter—all three rail-thin—in a tiny, one-room shanty just a few yards outside the fence around our hillside campus. His home had simple concrete blocks, a tin roof, a dirt floor, a mattress of sorts, a chair and a few odds and ends stacked in a corner. The odds and ends were hidden by a sheet hanging from the termite-eaten two-by-fours that held the tin roof in place.

Relatively new to this Port-au-Prince neighborhood and way of life, I often wondered how this too typical family survived. Over time, I began to feel free to ask questions about Henri's life. "How do you feed your family? Where do you find food?" He explained that it was unpredictable. Sometimes he found someone to pay him for simple, temporary work; other times a neighbor would have enough to share with them; perhaps a charitable passerby would give them something to eat; or sometimes they simply had nothing.

"What do you do all day?" He awoke each morning with no feasible plan and no assurance that a meal would be part of his day. "Is your daughter in school?" He couldn't afford it. "What happens when one of you gets sick?" They simply endured it. I finally was able to give him a simple job with very modest wages. He manned a gate on our campus. He tried to save a little money and improve his family's life, with the hope of enrolling his daughter in school. But after all his hard work, some neighborhood toughs robbed Henri's home, taking all his savings.

At the end of an extended summer trip back to the U.S. to visit family and friends, I learned that Henri had fallen ill and died. His wife and daughter were forced to leave the area in search of a way to survive.

This is not life as God designed it. In fact, what many Haitians and the majority of the world's population experience would be better labeled *death*, even for those who continue to breathe. It is precisely the opposite of God's design; it is anti-life.

How did this happen? Unfortunately, we have no one else to blame for it but ourselves. What the world is experiencing is the death that God warned Adam about in Genesis 2:16–17. Adam, I've given you all good things for your pleasure. Enjoy. But remember, life is from Me and depends on Me. Turn from Me and you will lose it—you can't find it elsewhere. Abandon Me and you abandon life. Seek life apart from Me and you will surely die.

God was not making a threat. He was issuing a gracious warning that, if heeded, would ensure Adam's joy. Sadly, Adam chose to listen to the evil one. You won't die. In fact, if you can manage to escape God's tyranny, you'll rise to His level. You'll be like Him, not under His thumb. You can chart your own course, set your own priorities, and make your own pleasure.

THE QUEST FOR LIFE

All of us are like Adam. We were created for life and we naturally yearn for it. We have an innate sense that the world is not as it is supposed to be, that there's something better out there. In a very real sense, we are all on a quest, striving to find a more satisfying, fulfilling existence, desperately thirsty for that elusive elixir that will take away the pain and make us happy.

Such was the reality of a Samaritan woman whose encounter with Jesus in John 4 powerfully illustrates this universal quest. Everyone knows what it's like to be thirsty and quench that thirst with a gulp of cool, clean

We have an innate sense that the world is not as it is supposed to be, that there's something better out there.

water. It's a universally experienced longing and relief. Is there any language that doesn't include a satisfied *ahhh* in its vocabulary?

Jesus masterfully uses that universal sensation to turn a seemingly simple request for a drink to a conversation about living water. It's an intriguing exchange in John 4 that begins with a tired Jesus resting by the well. When a woman comes to draw water, Jesus asks her:

"Will you give me a drink?"

"You are a Jew and I am a Samaritan woman. How can you ask me for a drink?" It was unheard of for a Jewish man to acknowledge a Samaritan woman, let alone speak to her.

"If you knew the gift of God and who it is that asks you for a drink, you would have asked him and he would have given you living water."

"Sir, you have nothing to draw with and the well is deep. Where can you get this living water? Are you greater than our father Jacob, who gave us the well and drank from it himself?" The woman believes she's doing just fine. She has what she needs to get her water, and the well she uses is specially made by Jacob.

Jesus answers, "Everyone who drinks this water will be thirsty again, but whoever drinks the water I give them will never thirst. Indeed, the water I give them will become in them a spring of water welling up to eternal life."

"Sir, give me this water so that I won't get thirsty and have to keep coming here to draw water."

The woman has no idea that Jesus is really offering to quench her deepest thirst. She had repeatedly gone to this well to satisfy her recurring thirst and agrees that it would be nice to be satisfied once and for all. But Jesus points her to a deeper thirst and to the ultimate satisfaction: "If you knew the gift of God, you would want it, you would ask me for it, and I would give it to you…and you would finally be satisfied." While "the gift of God" certainly includes the Spirit (John 7), the Son, and perhaps other aspects of salvation, Jesus is speaking primarily of that ultimately satisfying eternal gift of life.

DESPERATELY THIRSTY PEOPLE

Human beings spend their lives going to the well over and over again. We look for even better wells hoping for the most satisfying water. We are frighteningly relentless in our quest and will literally do whatever it takes to find satisfaction, pleasure, happiness or something—anything—that will make our existence better. I'm pursuing life. Get out of my way or get trampled.

When the band Gungor was nominated for Grammys in both 2010 and 2011, frontman Michael Gungor went to the awards ceremony wrestling with his feelings about the recognition that winning could bring. He shared some of his thoughts in *Christianity Today*, expressing the illusiveness of the human quest:

It is no secret that people worship celebrity in our culture. To be recognized as more special than others is a powerful feeling of love and acceptance. The problem is that this sort of recognition never satisfies. The feeling of worth that comes with the accolades of the crowd is shallow and fleeting. It is a counterfeit to real love and security.

Lust may have a lot of the same feelings associated with it that love does. Desire. Passion. Arousal. But lust is not love. It's a shallow and cheap counterfeit for love that never satisfies the soul; it only quiets the body for a moment. The pleasure from indulged lust is short-lived and shallow, but a life of true love is the richest and most satisfying life possible. Our true confidence and self-worth are rooted in the fact that we are the beloved of the Creator, fearfully and wonderfully made.[2]

Consider some of the things we do to quench our thirst for life. We steal and murder. We embezzle funds and abuse children. We have extra-marital affairs. We go to war. We rape. We lie. We cheat. We strap bombs to our bodies. We fly airplanes into skyscrapers. We offer sacrifices to spirits and pay intermediaries to put curses on our enemies. We pay women to take their clothes off and sell pictures of titillating sexual activity. We file fraudulent income tax returns. We put illegal substances in our bodies to outperform our competitors, and we ingest other drugs to provide moments of stuporous escape. We betray people to achieve greater power and wealth—wealth we can use to buy other attempts at satisfying pleasure.

I once heard the story of two childhood friends, Nick and Aaron, who grew up being as close as brothers. Later, when Nick married Aaron's younger sister, they became brothers-in-law. Nick owned a construction company that failed. So Aaron, whose own computer games company was thriving, stepped in to share his good fortune with his friend. He hired Nick as manager of the company's finances and computer systems.

How did Nick repay Aaron's kindness? He systematically stole nearly $9 million from the company over the next ten years, driving it to the brink of ruin. As the company inexplicably struggled in spite of relative market success, Aaron made deep staff reductions with three rounds of layoffs. He refused to take a paycheck for himself, mortgaged his home and sold his office building. He even emptied his retirement savings and poured the proceeds into saving his company. Meanwhile, Nick lived the secret life of a millionaire, enjoying his stolen wealth in ways that would not be easily noticed, all at the expense of Aaron and his family.

No human being is exempt from this thirsty quest for life. Just about everything we do is intended to somehow make our existence a little better and more meaningful.

Why would Nick do such a thing? Good question. Why would any of us do any of the despicable things I described above? The sad truth is that, having lost out on life as God intended it to be, we are desperately driven to quench that universal thirst for what's missing, even if we hurt others in the process.

No human being is exempt from this thirsty quest for life. Just about everything we do is intended to somehow make our existence a little better and more meaningful.

On a recent trip to India, I saw holy men who spend their lives sitting naked under a tree, covered in ash, dispensing insight they have gained through such rigors. Surely *they* are not pursuing pleasure and satisfaction, are they? Yes, they are. They have an innate sense that there is a way to greater meaning and contentment, and they're convinced that more conventional approaches will fail. They give up immediate comforts in their quest for even greater enlightenment and fulfillment.

Materialists, pornographers, existentialists, drug addicts, hedonists, Hindus, Buddhists, practitioners of Voodoo, Muslims and, dare I say, even many who call themselves Christians, set off on various paths in search of thirst-quenching life. Our creativity is quite astounding. You'd think we had tried it all by now, but the next guy comes along and thinks to himself, "Surely there must be a better way."

by JOHN BERGER, Crossworld's Vice President
for Global Operations and Strategy

CHAPTER / 08

LIFE AS IT WAS MEANT TO BE

For all of us seekers of a better way, there is incredible news. Let these words of Jesus sink in: "I have come that they may have life, and have it to the full" (John 10:10b, NIV).

We do not have to keep going back over and over again to wells that ultimately can never satisfy. To all who will come to Him, Jesus offers to restore life as it was meant to be.

I love how there are so many ways to describe the multiple facets of the good news of life offered to us by God. That fully satisfying, never-ending, pleasure-filled, thoroughly joyful, completely healthy, limitlessly prosperous, wonderfully beautiful life that God intended for us is ours for the taking. Mere words fail to capture it.

I'm baffled every time I realize how deeply God wants us to take hold of life and enjoy it. He wants it so deeply that He would actually be pleased for His Son to lay down His life. Yes, pleased. Jesus Himself says, "The reason my Father loves me is that I lay down my life—only to take it up again. No one takes it from me, but I lay it down of my own accord" (John 10:17–18, NIV). The prophet Isaiah made a similar statement some six hundred years before the crucifixion when he wrote, "But the LORD was pleased to crush Him, putting Him to grief, if He would render Himself as a guilt offering…" (Isaiah 53:10).

The nature of the Trinity is mysterious. The Father loves the Son for choosing to lay down His life so we might have life. It actually *pleased* God that His own Son be crushed! Just think of the lengths to which God would go—and did go—to give us the life He designed for us. The life we forfeited.

WHEN GOD SIGHS

While listening to the Gospel of Mark on my drive to the office, I was struck by two mentions of Jesus sighing. If I had noticed it before, it had somehow failed to register. In Mark 7, people brought a deaf mute to Jesus and begged Him to heal the man. While Jesus was going through some rather unique healing motions, He looked up to heaven and *with a deep sigh* said to the man, "Be opened" (v. 34; emphasis added). Then in Mark 8, some Pharisees came and began to question Jesus. To test Him, they asked Him for a sign from heaven. "*Sighing deeply* in His spirit, He said, 'Why does this generation seek for a sign?'" (v. 12; emphasis added).

Can you feel the heart of Jesus in those sighs? Two different situations—a physical handicap and unbelieving judgmental hearts. But a common frustration with the "not-right-ness" of the world. Jesus was vexed and frustrated—broken-hearted really—longing for His beloved creation to overcome the death that entered with our rebellion. Do you detect His pain? And can you sense the passion of His rescue mission? In order to spare us from a life of death, our Savior chose to come and lay down His very own life.

That is good news. And *good* is an understatement in this case.

Jesus hints that *life* is also an understatement. He is compelled to clarify that it is abundant life (John 10:10). But He doesn't stop there—He takes it up a notch and calls it "eternal life" in John 17:3. See the superlative progression? Life, abundant life, eternal life.

Jesus was vexed and frustrated—broken-hearted really—longing for His beloved creation to overcome the death that entered with our rebellion.

WHAT IS ETERNAL LIFE?

If I were to survey people in churches around the world and ask them the meaning of eternal life, what do you think they would say? I'm afraid many would settle for something such as *life without end*. Though their answer would be true, it would also be wholly inadequate. Eternal life is much more than unending existence. In fact, I believe that the duration aspect—though important, of course—is only secondary.

Jesus does not leave us to wonder what He means by eternal life. He defines it for us in His prayer in John 17:3. "This is eternal life, that they may know You, the only true God, and Jesus Christ whom You have sent." In a few short words, Jesus essentially brings us right back to the beginning in the Garden of Eden. Life, eternal life, life as it was meant to be, is to know God—fully, satisfyingly, perfectly. It is a perfect summation of everything I said in the previous chapter.

Let's review:

God created us that He might glorify Himself.

In glorifying Himself, God generously favors us with unspeakable-pleasure.

The joyful experience that God designed for us is called life—He created us for life.

The ultimate experience of life can be summed up in two words: knowing God.

The good news of life—abundant, eternal life—is that anyone who will receive the gift of God may experience the unimaginable satisfaction, fulfillment, joy, contentment, pleasure and grace of knowing Him. There is One and only One who far surpasses all others and all else, and He invites us to know Him and to enjoy Him and His creation forever.

THE WAY OF WISDOM

We who have already passed from death to life and are following Jesus have been commissioned to go to the nations, announce this good news, and assure people that the quest for life is legitimate. We are called to help others find life.

Proverbs 7 and 8 artfully present the necessary choice between two contrasting ways—one way leads to death and the other leads to life. These two ways are personified as women. The first one is called Adulteress. She lurks on the street corner, fetchingly dressed, seducing simple passers-by to come in and enjoy her pleasures: "I have good food at home, I have covered my bed with fine linens, and I have perfumed my bed with pleasing aromas. Come with me; let's enjoy ourselves all night long."

The other woman is Wisdom. She stands on a high spot at the city gates and cries out to everyone she sees. She pleads with them to listen to her and to not be deceived by alternative invitations to well being: "Listen, for I have worthy things to say; I open my lips to speak what is right. My fruit is better than fine gold!" She ends her discourse in Proverbs 8 with these startling words: "For those who find me find life and receive favor from the Lord. But those who fail to find me harm themselves; *all who hate me love death*" (Proverbs 8:35–36, NIV; emphasis added).

What a stark contrast! One way seems quite attractive and provides significant pleasure. But in comparison to the better way, those pleasures are inferior. And what's worse, the path of the adulteress ultimately leads to death. It's the path Adam chose. It's the path we often choose. It's the futile and ignorant quest for life apart from God. Those who follow it are deprived of the very thing they long to experience.

Carrie grew up attending church. She learned a lot about eternal life in church, but she believed that it all applied to a mysterious afterlife, not so much to her experience on earth. As a twenty-one-year-old seeking to have a life, she worked downtown as a cocktail waitress. She would drink every night, do drugs, and routinely engage in sexual relationships with different men. She had to take medication on top of the recreational drugs in order to sleep at night, but she loved it. Or so she thought.

"I thought I was having the time of my life," she recounts. "That is, until my life started to crumble." She began to realize that none of her friends were true friends. She would lie in bed after a very long night of partying and worry about the trajectory of her life and the debt she had gotten herself into. Her growing unhappiness spawned a determination to change her lifestyle, but she couldn't seem to do it. "Every night I would tell myself that I was going to stay sober. Instead, I would pull another all-nighter with my 'friends' and come home at 10 a.m. feeling disappointed and ashamed."

At the darkest point of her life, her brother excitedly shared with her the good news he had just discovered about Jesus. The Lord opened her eyes, and as she puts it, "I was reborn!" She decided to follow Jesus and found herself empowered to leave the self-destructive path she had chosen. "The memories of that first year of new life are so precious and dear to me. I have never felt so loved in my life; I could feel God pouring His love on me."

Carrie chose the way of wisdom and experienced a radical transformation. Now seven years later, she is healthy, married, has two lovely children with a third on the way, and she is growing in maturity. She and her husband have joined Crossworld and are nearing departure for Southeast Asia, eager to share with hurting people the life they discovered in Jesus.

The gospel that Jesus sent His disciples to preach is none other than a call to choose the way of wisdom, the way of life, the way of Jesus. There is a right way to live, a right way to be, and a right way to think…and this right way is part of the good news that transforms lives and communities. The good news invites us to take hold of the life God designed and intended for us. And when we live that way, we flourish. Families are healed. Communities are transformed. The way of wisdom is the way of life.

Imagine the health of communities where people value their neighbor's well-being more than their own wealth; where husbands encourage, love and remain faithful to their wives rather than complaining about them and seeking intimacy elsewhere; where families respect and honor their aging parents; and where business is conducted honestly. Imagine people for whom caring for the poor is just a natural reaction to seeing their pain. There is a right way to live—the way of wisdom—and *it leads to life*.

A graduate of our Haitian seminary accepted the leadership of a small church in an impoverished community in the arid northwest region of Haiti. As he persistently taught and modeled "the way," a band of maturing disciples began to see their community with new eyes. Over time their village, which had no water, no health care (other than the local witchdoctor) and very poor educational opportunities, began to experience change. Working together with believers in neighboring areas and outside agencies, this community worked to establish a fresh water source, a thriving school and a simple clinic/pharmacy to care for the sick.

A Crossworld colleague in Ecuador told Gustavo's story. After Gustavo decided to follow Jesus Christ, his friends noticed a change of attitude as he stopped using foul language. He then began to notice his own economic situation improving—his salary as a security guard at night and a shoemaker during the day suddenly stretched farther. He was no longer spending his money on alcohol, cigarettes and prostitutes. His family life changed completely! No longer pursuing other "interests" at the bars and dance halls, he had time to take them to the park and to participate in church activities. And now his daughter's grades have been rapidly improving, and his wife has joined him in studying the Bible. Gustavo also meets with my colleague twice a week and is soaking up everything he can from the Word. He has found a better way to live.

There is a right way to live—the way of wisdom—and it leads to life.

The apostle Paul was a fervent disciple-maker who mentored Timothy, among others. In a letter to his dear friend, Paul encouraged Timothy to help people recognize counterfeit offers of life: "Instruct those who are rich in this present world not to be conceited or to fix their hope on the uncertainty of riches, but on God, who richly supplies us with all things to enjoy. Instruct them to do good, to be rich in good works, to be generous and ready to share, storing up for themselves the treasure of a good foundation for the future, so that they may take hold of *that which is life indeed*" (1 Timothy 6:17–19; emphasis added). In other words, Timothy, tell them the better way.

TRANSFORMED LIFE, TRANSFORMED WORLD

When we chose *A Better Way* as part of Crossworld's tagline and as the title for this book, we were well aware that some might misunderstand it, thinking we were either suggesting Crossworld as the better way or claiming that previous methodologies were inferior to what we envision for the future.

Likewise, our "better way" message is not born out of an attitude of superiority or condemnation, but out of a longing for the world to know life as it was meant to be.

In a similar way, the gospel message can be sometimes misunderstood as a put-down of other faiths, as if to say, "Our religion is better than your religion. Join us or perish in hell."

But Jesus came neither to institute a new religion nor to condemn an old one. He came to offer life! "For God did not send the Son into the world to judge the world, but that the world might be saved through Him" (John 3:17).

Likewise, our "better way" message is not born out of an attitude of superiority or condemnation, but out of a longing for the world to know life as it was meant to be and to see the carriers of Jesus' abundant life multiplied throughout the world in our lifetime.

The message of "a better way" is really two-fold. For those who have yet to discover a transformed life, the better way is Jesus—not money, not stuff, not power or passion or position or popularity or any other dry well that humanity attempts to drink from, but Jesus, who offers true life!

And for those who have experienced a transformed life and long for a transformed world, the better way is still Jesus and His way. This means *making disciples*, not just converts; *sending all professions*, not just the religious profession; and *offering abundant life now*, not just proclaiming eternal life for later.

THIS IS *THE BETTER WAY*

At Crossworld, the sheer goodness of the good news of Jesus compels us to never stop pursuing *better ways* to convey it.

George Malley's experience was a short-lived, sensational phenomenon. And it was fictional. So why did it stir in me such anticipation of…something? Because I know both intuitively and theologically that humanity was designed for so much more. It is said that truth is stranger than fiction. But as it relates to the wonder of the good news of life, we'd have to say that truth is more *phenomenal* than fiction. I can barely imagine what awaits us in eternity future (George Malley and then some!), and I'm afraid I fail to grasp just how satisfying the miniscule taste of that future could be even now. But we can grasp enough to be driven to offer that life to the people for whom God designed it.

CHAPTER 09

THROWING OPEN THE SHUTTERS ON THE 925 WINDOW

I have a dream. I dream of a world where disciple-making is a reality and not just an ideal; where disciples make disciples who make disciples and unleash the explosive power of spiritual multiplication.

I dream of a world where every believer embraces his call and every profession is employed in the cause to disciple the nations; where cross-cultural disciple-makers from secular professions outnumber vocational Christian workers one hundred to one.

I dream of a world where the church is not defined as a building, program or number of Christians, but as fervent followers of Christ on a mission to extend the kingdom of God.

I dream of a world where the good news of Jesus impacts not just a person's eternity, but all of life here and now.

I dream of a world in which every city has a vibrant community of reproducing disciple-makers who will permeate all of society like yeast permeates dough.

And I dream of a world in which a Christian is known as a lover of God, people and life.

In short, I dream of *disciple-makers from all professions bringing God's love to life in the world's least-reached marketplaces.* That is the dream we at Crossworld are committed to pursuing with all our heart. That is the dream that we also long for others to embrace.

As I've already explained in preceding chapters, it is first and foremost a dream of unleashing the power of real disciple-making. It is based on the conviction that this is exactly what Jesus told us to do, and if we do it, the Great Commission would be completed in our lifetime.

But it is also a dream of unleashing the power of all believers. It is a dream that believes the former way of mobilizing mostly religious professionals to go to the nations is not enough—that there is a better way: mobilizing *all* professionals.

ENGAGING GODLY PROFESSIONALS TO DISCIPLE THE NATIONS

If you have had much to do with the missionary movement over the past twenty years, you will probably recognize the term *10/40 Window.* It was coined by missionary strategist Luis Bush in 1990 and refers to the regions of the Eastern Hemisphere located between ten and forty degrees north of the equator and having the highest concentration of least-reached people on the planet.

While many are familiar with the 10/40 Window, surprisingly few have heard of another unreached group of people living in a zone called the *925 Window.* Let me describe it to you. It's a window virtually all believers look through almost every day of their lives—many of them without ever realizing it. Many, in fact, view it as more of a window with bars, a prison cell, rather than what it really is—a huge window of opportunity. Personally, I don't live in the 925 Window—at least not in the one that most people experience.

Most of my days from 9 a.m. to 5 p.m. are spent working at a place called Crossworld. It's a great place to work, but the view is quite limited. I work with about thirty people—all of them followers of Jesus, and very fine ones, I might add. I also spend a good number of my weekends with similar groups of fine people, speaking at local churches or conferences. Several times a year I travel internationally, again, usually to spend time with more wonderful people—missionaries, as they are often called.

By now perhaps you understand that the 925 Window is the window of opportunity that most believers have from 9 a.m. to 5 p.m. every day, to be salt and light in an unbelieving world. It is a natural window of opportunity that allows us to enter the ordinary world of people that Jesus came to seek and save.

Do you see 925 as a window of opportunity? Or do you view your job as a prison cell that you'd love to be liberated from so you could *really* serve God? The fact is, the 925 Window is a God-given opportunity we need to wake up to.

WHO REALLY IS CALLED TO FULL-TIME MINISTRY?

Though most would say that someone like me is in full-time ministry, I would beg to differ. I cringe when I hear a pastor or missionary talk about being "called to full-time ministry" as if it is one step between earth and heaven. I actually think that people like me have, in a sense, been taken *out* of full-time ministry. If you live and work in the secular world, *you* are the one in full-time ministry. You are the expert at relating to 99 percent of the world. You are the one in touch.

Scripture explicitly states that it is the job of people like me (pastors and teachers) to equip people like you "for the work of service" (Ephesians 4:12). Believers are to be prepared for *ministry.* Certainly the ministry world of the average follower of Jesus encompasses more than teaching a forty-five-minute Sunday school class or ushering other believers to their pews on Sunday morning. The ministry world is the 925 Window!

Many believers working in the secular world do not view themselves as involved in ministry. And whose fault is that? Perhaps those who have fostered the false dichotomy between work and ministry need to shoulder some of the blame.

While those who work in the secular world are in touch with people from all walks of life, I have to go to great lengths not to be out of touch! Since I work with believers all day long, I have to go out of my way to rub shoulders with regular folks. I have to do things like getting up extra early on snow days to help my neighbor shovel his driveway. Or finding out about the guy behind the counter at my favorite café in hope that I can eventually get together with him for lunch and go a little deeper.

The 925 Window is one of the most overlooked, untapped ministry opportunities in the world. I would submit to you that the workplace in North America and beyond is the most strategic place of ministry for most of Christ's followers.

The dichotomous notion that religious work is ministry and secular work is not has been very harmful. It has for too long insulted the body of Christ and handicapped the advance of the gospel. It has communicated to the unbelieving world that faith in God has little to do with life.

Speaking of the tragic disconnect between the world and the church, author Dorothy Sayers laments, "How can anyone remain interested in a religion which seems to have no concern with nine-tenths of life?"[1] The 925 Window is one of the most overlooked, untapped ministry opportunities in the world. I would submit to you that the workplace in North America and beyond is the most strategic place of ministry for most of Christ's followers. It is where we find the hurting and the lost. And for the vast majority of people, it is their main hub of relationships.

SOME OF THE GREAT 925ERS

Some of the greatest world changers in history were 925ers. R.G. LeTourneau, whose story is told in the book *Mover of Men and Mountains*, was one such man. As the father of the modern earth-moving industry and founder of LeTourneau University, his influence was far reaching. The spiritual impact of his life dwarfs the mere impact of building a successful earth-moving company.[2]

On the other side of the Atlantic, William Wilberforce was another powerful 925er who initially wrestled with the issue of secular versus sacred work. This member of British Parliament, together with American President Abraham Lincoln, was instrumental in the abolition of slavery. Having embraced the evangelical faith, Wilberforce found himself on what he considered the horns of a dilemma. He had to decide whether to stay in politics or to serve God in "full-time ministry."

Michael Metzger of The Clapham Institute (an organization that studies the DNA of organizations) notes, "Wilberforce was dividing the world between higher and lower callings; between sacred and secular work. It's what Os Guinness calls the 'Catholic distortion,' which goes all the way back to church leaders like Eusebius, Augustine, and Aquinas. Monks, nuns, and priests 'had a calling'—they performed 'spiritual work.' Soldiers, farmers, and business people 'just had jobs'—they were stuck with 'secular' work. By Wilberforce's day, many evangelicals had adopted the Catholic distortion…."[3]

The dilemma, powerfully depicted in the movie *Amazing Grace,* was finally resolved for Wilberforce one evening over dinner with a unique group of believers who had given themselves to social reform. When the question of Wilberforce's indecision between politics and ministry was raised, one wise member of the group replied, "We humbly suggest that you can do both."[4]

Biblical history abounds with godly men and women from secular professions who impacted the world for all eternity. Though Daniel is often considered a religious worker because of his prophetic role, he was far more than that. He was a godly career politician who served under three successive world rulers and, in the process, gave us the most astoundingly detailed end-time prophecies of any Old Testament writer.

David was another. He wrote a significant chunk of the Scriptures, but not as a religious professional. He was a politician, a military leader, and one of the greatest rulers of all time. Solomon was another godly man who was not only a political ruler but arguably one of the wisest men ever to live. The list goes on of men and women like Joseph, Moses, Joshua, Ruth, Esther, Nehemiah and more. They impacted their world not by leaving it to become "full-time" workers, but by serving God using the unique skills and professional roles God had entrusted to them.

Whether God has called you to a career of politics, business, social work or any other vocation, realize this: *God has called you.* You serve Him best when you serve Him through the unique skills and passions He has given you.

LIVING IN THE 925 WINDOW

Today, with few exceptions, the majority of the world's least-reached places with the highest concentration of non-Christian religions are places that will not allow you to enter as a religious worker. There are at least seventy such countries in the world today, and the number is growing. More than four billion people today live in countries where vocational Christian workers (missionaries) are no longer admitted (see Appendix). Many of these areas of the world with evangelical populations of less than 1 percent represent the largest and most spiritually needy part of the 925 Window in our world today.

Let me paint a picture of one such place for you.

The Ganges River, lovingly referred to by Hindus as "Our Mother," snakes its way along the Ganges Plain, home to four hundred million people who live along its path. When I visited there four years ago, I climbed into an old wooden boat in Varanasi for a one-hour paddle along the Ganges. Varanasi is the holiest city in India. Each day sixty thousand people go down to one of the *ghats* (stairways descending to the Ganges River) to take a holy dip along this four-mile stretch that runs through the city. Along this same area, thirty large sewers continuously discharge into the river. The waters are so heavily polluted that the World Health Organization classifies it as an environmental hazard. Water is considered safe for swimming if it has fewer than five hundred fecal coliform bacteria per one hundred milliliters of water. In Varanasi, the water's measurement per unit is *1.5 million* fecal parts!

Pilgrims come from all over the country to wash in this water. Many Hindus want to die in Varanasi because they believe doing so guarantees liberation from the endless cycle of birth and death. The elderly and sick come, sometimes being carried off trains, to die in the streets or in a hospice of this holy place.

One small section of the *ghat*, I observed, was a microcosm of life along the Ganges River. Five women stood side by side in the space of about twenty feet. One was performing her ritual washing. The second was washing her clothes. The third was scrubbing her pots and pans. The fourth was cleaning her teeth using her finger and a mouthful of water. And the last one was patting manure into flat cakes and setting them out to dry in the sun to be used for cooking purposes. Just upriver from these women was the place where bodies were cremated and their ashes thrown into the river.

Never had I seen such an endless and seemingly hopeless spiritual quest. The people were ringing bells, offering flowers, kissing the toes of idols, pouring drink offerings on the roots of trees, burning incense, chanting prayers, and even bathing in raw sewage.

Today I can pray for God to send workers into that harvest, but I cannot go because my seminary degree does not offer me any way of entry to live or work in that land or many others like it.

But thankfully there are those who can help.

One of them is a young photographer. His parents are veteran cross-cultural workers who successfully established numerous churches in one of Crossworld's historic ministry areas. We asked them if they would consider moving to a new part of the world to spearhead a team of 925ers. Having come from a traditional Bible college background, they had no professional entry point. None, that is, until their son came along.

Phil is a great photographer who was already earning his living doing photography in the U.S. Why couldn't he develop his business in an Asian setting and provide the same or better service to his North American clientele at a reduced cost? So, together with his parents, he launched a successful business venture. It allows all three of them to live and work in a least-reached part of the world, doing legitimate, profitable business with a disciple-making purpose. What better way to reach the unreached than to do it by going to their world rather than making them come to ours? What better way to reach a businessman than to be a businessman?

What better way to impact a place where unemployment runs as high as 30 percent than to start a business that provides a way for employees to put food on the table for their families?

The world is not closed to us if we are willing to change our means of engagement. In fact, in more and more cases, people are delighted to welcome us because of the tangible difference our lives bring to theirs.

This was the case for another 925er who recently moved to the other side of the world to make disciples by means of a tourism business. The local authorities were so pleased to learn that he was interested in stimulating tourism in their country that they took him on a tour of the region, putting him up in five-star hotels at their own expense. Does it matter to them that he is a follower of Jesus? Not if he is there to do legitimate business in their country. Can he stand on the street corner preaching the gospel? Not unless he wants his visa revoked. But most likely, street-corner preaching is not the best way to share the gospel in that culture anyway.

The world is not closed to us if we are willing to change our means of engagement.

For the better part of two centuries, Western evangelicalism has championed the model of *proclamation and invitation* by a religious professional. Typically, unbelievers have been invited to venture onto Christian turf (i.e. our church building) once or twice a year on Christmas, Easter or "Bring-a-Friend Day." They listen to a full-time, religious professional proclaim a message and are then invited to accept it.

The more stouthearted among us will sometimes take that message to the streets and proclaim it with a tract or some kind of gospel-based performance. But the approach is essentially the same—either proclaiming truth from the safety of *our* world or making a brief foray into their world to give them a message that, to them, seems out of sync with the rest of life.

While those approaches have certainly yielded some results, I would suggest that they are increasingly ineffective and inaccessible to the majority of lost people today. There is a better way than proclaiming the truth from our world. It's *living and proclaiming* the truth in their world.

One way is *invitational.* The better way is *incarnational.* One way focuses on proclamation by the religious professional. The better way calls for incarnation by believers of all professions.

A NEW KIND OF MISSIONARY

I dream of a new kind of missionary working side by side with traditional ones like me. I dream of godly men and women who know what it means to make a disciple and believe that God has called them to do so using their unique training, gifting or experience.

We need *ground-breakers* who will enter a new least-reached marketplace ahead of the rest of the team to seek out solid business and professional opportunities and craft strategies for the team members who will follow.

We also need *business developers, profession-based disciple-makers, ministry team leaders,* and *vocational cross-cultural workers*, like me, whose experience and training lend itself to a more focused attention on the spiritual development of team members and new disciples.

And in North America, we need a host of *godly business and professional partners.*

LOSING FOR JESUS

Some have said to me, "I think you're going to have a hard time finding business and professional people who will leave what they have here to do what you're talking about." Their reasoning goes something like this: it's hard enough to find vocational religious workers to go overseas. What business person or successful young professional would give up a career, an American-sized income and the comforts of life to go live and work in some crowded city of Asia, North Africa or Europe?

Such reasoning grossly underestimates the body of Christ. As I share the vision of *A Better Way*, I am encountering more and more godly professionals who are ready for the challenge. In his excellent book *Radical Together*, author and pastor David Platt writes, "The church is a community of individuals who have lost their lives to follow Christ."[5] If that is indeed the case (and I believe it is), why would anyone question whether such individuals would embrace the cause of taking God's glory to the nations? Platt goes on to tell story after story of men and women who are

The only people who would sign up for the kind of dream that I've been describing are disciples willing to lose their lives so that others might find life.

doing just that—selling possessions, adopting children, or moving their families and careers to dangerous parts of the world.

I met such a woman recently. She had spent her entire career in the business world. Her life had been radically transformed through an encounter with Jesus when she was in her early fifties. A few years ago, at age sixty, this widow, mother and grandmother caught a vision for the impoverished women of India. She subsequently liquidated her assets, retired from the professional world, and moved to one of the world's least-reached marketplaces. For the past three years, she has been making disciples by means of micro-enterprise and community development.

Who in their right mind would leave behind loved ones, a career and a comfortable lifestyle to spend not only their retirement years but their own resources for such a cause? You need only look into the tear-filled eyes of this beautiful woman of God to have your answer: those who have lost their lives for Jesus and the gospel—in other words, mature disciples. A disciple is one who is *learning to live and love like Jesus and helps others to do the same.* Such a person, by Jesus' own definition, is characterized by LOSS—love, obedience *and self-sacrifice.*

The only people who would sign up for the kind of dream that I've been describing are disciples willing to lose their lives so that others might find life. The kind of person I'm talking about is someone like the man Jesus described in a parable. After finding a treasure hidden in a field, he sold everything he had to acquire the field and its hidden treasure.

If this describes you, if like this man you're so captivated by the abundant life you've found in Jesus that you can't fathom keeping it to yourself when you know that there are places and people who have yet to discover what real life is all about, then I urge you to pursue the dream. Real life. Once you've found how good it really is, keeping it to yourself is really not an option.

CHAPTER 10

WHAT ABOUT THE CHURCH?

With all this talk about disciple-making and a new kind of missionary, you might be wondering what has happened to the church. Am I suggesting we abandon church planting in favor of disciple-making? And are secular professionals going to completely replace vocational religious workers?

Let me be absolutely clear on this. Christ loves the church and gave Himself up for it. We can do no less. We are fully committed to the establishment of new churches—disciple-making communities that are committed to extending Christ's kingdom. And engaging all believers from all professions is a complement to, not a replacement of, vocational Christian workers.

I once spoke to a group of church leaders about the need to engage the whole body of Christ in making disciples of the nations. One of those in attendance questioned my commitment to the church. His reasoning went something like this: "You talk a lot about disciple-makers from all professions, but where's the church in all of this? How can you expect business and professional people to have time for ministry or the training needed to do the real work of establishing the church?"

DOES GOD USE UNTRAINED PEOPLE?

How did Jesus establish the church? Whom did He use to make disciples and launch new communities of faith? I wonder if we have forgotten the rather humble beginnings of the church.

Engaging all believers from all professions is a complement to, not a replacement of, vocational Christian workers.

You may recall that very shortly after the day of Pentecost, when the number of believers was expanding at a rate almost too rapid to count, two of the three top leaders of this fledgling church were detained for questioning by the religious authorities. As Peter and John stood before the Sanhedrin, they boldly defended their faith in the risen Lord. So much so that as the council members "observed the confidence of Peter and John and understood that they were uneducated and untrained men, they were amazed, and began to recognize them as having been with Jesus" (Acts 4:13).

Did you catch that? Whom did Jesus use to establish the very first church? *Uneducated and untrained men!* They hadn't been to rabbinical school, Bible college or seminary. They had no degrees after their names. They were just ordinary guys. In fact, they were *uneducated*, ordinary guys. But they had been with Jesus, been taught by Him, and been discipled by Him through the transmission of God's truth in the context of life.

If they could be entrusted with the responsibility of making disciples and gathering them into local communities of faith, why should it be any different today? What resources did those men have then that we don't have today? They had the Old Testament. We have the Old *and* New Testaments! They had Jesus with them as a teacher. We have something even better! Better? What could possibly be better than having Jesus with you as your teacher? I'll tell you—having the indwelling Spirit of Jesus living in you as your teacher!

We are committed to sending the best that the church has to offer: godly, Spirit-filled believers from all professions—including vocational Christian workers.

Just before Jesus left, He said this to His followers: "But I tell you the truth, it is to your advantage that I go away…" (John 16:7). I can just imagine them thinking, "Are you kidding, Jesus? How could having You leave us be to our advantage?" Jesus added, "…for if I do not go away, the Helper will not come to you; but if I go, I will send Him to you…. But when He, the Spirit of truth, comes, He will guide you into all the truth; for He will not speak on His own initiative, but whatever He hears, He will speak; and He will disclose to you what is to come. He will glorify Me, for He will take of Mine and will disclose it to you" (John 16:7, 13–14).

God is not limited today to using seminary-educated and trained men and women to make disciples and establish His church any more than He was when He first launched the church. He has never made that a prerequisite. Rather, God uses spiritually gifted people, seminary-trained or not, to build His church. As Paul tells us in Ephesians 4, God gave apostles and prophets, pastors and teachers to equip the saints for ministry. We don't know if the early church training was formal or, as in the case of the apostles, primarily informal, truth saturated and experience based. But what was and still is essential is that disciple-makers be so full of God's Word and His Spirit that they are recognized as having been with Jesus.

It is not a question of sending more people who are less qualified. We at Crossworld are not interested in sending good businessmen and women who are weak Christians. We are committed to sending the best that the church has to offer: godly, Spirit-filled believers from all professions—including vocational Christian workers. Partnering together, they will make disciple-makers who will be the church.

The Spirit of God and the Word of God poured out through the people of God is totally sufficient for the establishment of the church throughout the world. If we think that ordinary Spirit-filled men and women today are incapable of making disciples and establishing the church, then we are seriously underestimating either the body of Christ or the transforming power of God's Word and Spirit.

WHEN DOES LIFE BEGIN?

Is a disciple-making emphasis missing the real goal? Isn't our focus supposed to be on church planting? It seems to me that this line of reasoning reveals another unhealthy dichotomy that has crept into the church.

Let me explain.

Most of us are quite familiar with the ongoing debate in our society between the pro-life and pro-choice movements. One of the questions that lies at the very heart of the issue is this: When does life begin? It's a simple question with profound implications for both mother and unborn child. A conviction that life begins at conception rather than at birth dramatically elevates the value we place on the unborn child.

So what are the implications of this question when applied to our disciple-making mandate? When does life begin in the disciple-making/

church-planting continuum?

For starters, we need to establish that this is in fact a *continuum*. To give you a picture of what I mean, allow me to expand on a concept I introduced in Chapter 3.

Disciple-making is to church planting what cell multiplication is to the development of a new living being. Disciple-making and church planting are meant to be part of a seamless process that ultimately results in the birth of a living being made up of living cells. The church is the living being. Disciples are the living cells. These are not separate processes; they are one. The reason Jesus told us to "go and make disciples" promising "I will build My church" rather than explicitly telling us to "make disciples *and* plant the church," is because the one assumes the other. Reproductive disciple-making that doesn't result in the establishment and growth of healthy churches is not biblical disciple-making.

Disciple-making and church planting are meant to be part of a seamless process that ultimately results in the birth of a living being made up of living cells. The church is the living being. Disciples are the living cells. These are not separate processes; they are one.

Consider what happens in the development of a brand new human being. The fertilized egg forms a cell that has all the genetic information necessary for the development of a new life. Immediately the cell begins multiplying—first two, then four, eight, sixteen, thirty-two and so on. When does that multi-celled organism become a living being? When it has a hundred, a thousand or a million cells? Is it when a fetal heartbeat can be detected at week six of development? Or is it at the end of week seven when everything that is present in an adult human is present in the developing embryo? Do the parents only think of it as a real baby when they can finally see all its body parts on the ultrasound? Or not until the fetus actually passes through the birth canal? When does that little human being actually become a human being? Though a twelve- to fifteen-week-old fetus is not yet a fully developed human being, it *is* fully a human being (albeit in embryonic form).

So when does a church become fully a church? Is it when there are two disciples who are mutually committed to each other's spiritual development? Or is it when there are four, eight or sixteen believers in attendance? Is it only once it has developed enough that one can actually know the people behind the head, hands and feet? Is it when the elder has been named an elder and the deacon a deacon? Or is it only when the church has been clothed with an official meeting place?

As soon as the Spirit of God penetrates one human heart and regeneration occurs, an "embryo" has been formed, and the seed of a new community of faith (or the growth of an existing one) begins. When that disciple multiplies to two, then four, eight and sixteen disciples, the embryonic form of a new community of faith—the church—results.

A strong commitment to this healthy, reproductive disciple-making does not make me "disciple-centric" as opposed to "church-centric." It makes me *life-centric.* It makes me (I hope), *Jesus-centric.*

Reproductive disciple-making (or spiritual multiplication) is the key to establishing healthy churches. The body is only as good as its cells, and the church is only as good as its disciples.

In his book *Jesus Christ: Disciplemaker*, Bill Hull writes, "I have not mellowed in my belief that making disciples is indeed the primary and exclusive work of the church. The fact that the church is weaker than ever and shrinking is the evidence that we still haven't got it."[1] In a similar vein, in the article "We Aren't About Weekends," Pastor Bob Roberts observed, "If you focus on mission, churches will follow, but if you focus on churches, mission often gets lost."[2]

At Crossworld, we have chosen to focus on the mandate Jesus gave us to make disciples who make disciples. We have chosen to do so out of love for Christ and His church. And we believe that if we focus on this mission, communities of disciples will begin to develop, individual members and roles will become progressively evident, and healthy "bodies" (churches) will be born.

CHAPTER 11

GOING WHERE THE PEOPLE ARE

Something unprecedented happened in the year 2000. For the first time in history, the majority of the world's population was living in urban areas. The explosion of urban populations is a very new phenomenon. For most of history, the population of the world was predominantly rural. In 1800, only 3 percent of humanity lived in cities. Even by 1900, it still stood at a modest 14 percent. Between 1900 and 2000, the world's population roughly quadrupled, from a little more than 1.5 billion to 6 billion. But what has been truly astonishing is that, in the last few decades of the twentieth century, migration to the cities kicked into high gear. And the momentum will only continue to accelerate. Estimates based on current trends point to 80 percent of the world's population living in cities by the year 2050. *Every week*, 1.3 million people (or 70 million per year) move to the city.

Not only are more and more people moving to cities, but the cities themselves are exploding in size. In 1950, there were eighty-three cities worldwide with populations in excess of one million. By 2007, that number had risen to 468. Projections indicate that the number will reach 650 by the year 2025. Megacities have been defined as metropolitan areas with populations in excess of ten million. There are currently twenty-one such cities in the world today, most of them in Asia and Africa. Lagos, Nigeria, is an example of the explosive growth of these cities. Its population has grown from 300,000 in 1950 to an estimated 12.5 million today and a projected 25 million by 2015! On the continent of Africa alone, in the ten-year period between 1990 and 2000, the urban population nearly doubled from 130 million to 240 million.

The April 10, 2010, issue of *Financial Times* published a massive survey on the future of cities, describing the emergence of what they call *metacities*—cities with populations more than twenty million. Mexico City, with thirty-one million people, is an example of this. An astounding fourteen million people in that city are slum-dwellers, and half of the total population of the city is under thirteen years of age. Metacities, far larger than megacities, will be almost exclusively non-Western, and will include such places as Tokyo, Mumbai, Shanghai, Jakarta, Beijing, Karachi, São Paulo, Mexico City and Lagos.

A BETTER WAY TO REACH THE WORLD

For most of my life, the dominant image of cross-cultural missions was largely rural or tribal in nature. Being a missionary meant leaving the modern conveniences of life as we knew it and living like the natives in some remote place, usually without running water or electricity.

I remember the first time it really dawned on me that the world of cross-cultural missions was rapidly morphing into something very different than my stereotypical notions. I was in Senegal, exploring new ministry opportunities with a small group of leaders. We had driven from the capital of Dakar to visit a group of believers that was meeting in a smaller town about two hours away. We were waiting for people to arrive when up rode a man with his cart and horse. "How charming," I thought to myself, pondering how much more advanced things were in the bustling city of Toronto.

The world is moving to the city and is being united by technology, business, travel and a thirst for a common language in ways unprecedented since the Roman Empire.

As I stood there, I heard a cell phone ring and watched in astonishment as my "charming" African brother whipped out his cell phone to answer the call. I couldn't believe my eyes! Being one of the last holdouts in my circle of friends to make the switch to the wireless world, *I* didn't even own a cell phone yet! And there I was, watching someone in what I considered to be the underdeveloped world leapfrog right over me.

We are living in a very different world today, both demographically and technologically, than we were only a few short years ago. The world is moving to the city and is being united by technology, business, travel and a thirst for a common language in ways unprecedented since the Roman Empire.

While I would in no way minimize the continued need for tribal and rural ministry, I believe the most strategic place for the majority of Western cross-cultural disciple-makers today is in the great cities of the world. In the past, Westerners have almost single-handedly pioneered taking the gospel to the uttermost parts of the earth. In light of today's world, I believe there's a better way to reach the uttermost parts than to do it single-handedly. It involves equipping disciple-makers *in the world's least-reached urban marketplaces* to permeate society to the uttermost parts.

RURAL URBANITES

Lest you think this is a radical departure from the biblical way of doing missions, believe it or not the earliest missionary endeavors were almost strictly urban-focused.

Even before Paul arrived on the scene, the gospel thrust was urban. Acts chapters 1–12 trace the progress of the gospel from Jerusalem to Antioch. Notice the route that it took. It started in *Jerusalem*, the capital city of the Jewish nation. After persecution broke out in Jerusalem, we learn that Philip went down to the city of *Samaria* (Acts 8:3), where a great number were added to the faith.

He was then led out into the desert. Why? To develop a rural ministry? No. He was sent there because there was a high-ranking, God-seeking government official from the capital city of *Ethiopia*, who was on his way home (Acts 8:27). God was in the process of planting a new disciple in another major city. After that experience, Philip goes back to *Azotas* and surrounding towns. Azotas was the ancient Ashdod, one of the original five principal Philistine cities.

Next we find the church in *Damascus* (Acts 9:2), the principal city of Syria. The church was apparently sizable enough to draw the attention of Saul of Tarsus, who went there seeking to stamp it out.

Toward the end of Acts 9, we find that the church had spread to *Lydda*, *Sharon* and *Joppa*, all significant cities in the region. Joppa, for instance, was the principal seaport of Judea.

Next, the church is born in *Caesarea* (Acts 10:1). Named in honor of Caesar, Caesarea was the principal Roman city of the region and headquarters for the occupying Roman force.

Antioch was next on the list. Some unnamed witnesses who had been forced out of Jerusalem ministered there.

So before Paul even comes on the scene, the church has been established in all the principal cities of Palestine and even beyond. We can see clearly that the strategy of the early church was almost exclusively urban in nature.

The apostle Paul, who was arguably the most successful missionary ever, also had a decidedly urban-centered ministry. He went to all the major urban centers of the Roman Empire, including *Paphos*, *Perga*, *Antioch*, *Iconium*, *Lystra*, *Derbe*, *Ephesus*, *Philippi*, *Corinth* and more. The list of cities he visited goes on and on.

So successful was he in his mission, that when Paul came to the city of *Thessalonica* his opponents said, "These men who have *upset the world* have come here also…" (Acts 17:6b; emphasis added). How did Paul and his friends have such a far-reaching impact? The answer is simple: by focusing on disciple-making in the great cities of the world.

As other cultures and religions have invaded our cities, evangelical Christians have consistently moved further and further away from them.

Author Tim Keller has taught extensively on the strategic priority of reaching the city. He explains that by the year 300 A.D., more than half of the urban populations of the Roman Empire were Christian, while the countryside was pagan. The word *paganus* means *country-man*. So pagans were those who lived in the country.

Today, just the opposite is true in America. As other cultures and religions have invaded our cities, evangelical Christians have consistently moved further and further away from them. As Keller says, "This is a recipe for total cultural irrelevance!"[1]

Today in many parts of the world, cities are dominated not by followers of Jesus but by the *paganus.* What we have today are cities full of "rural urbanites." This should not be.

AS GOES THE CITY, SO GOES THE WORLD

Why do we believe that North Americans who sense God leading them to make disciples cross-culturally need to seriously consider the great urban marketplaces of the world? First, and most obviously, because that's where all the people are! We need to be where life is happening. But it goes beyond that.

The overriding example of Scripture is one of moving among urban populations in search of those in whom the Spirit of God is at work, then proclaiming God's truth, establishing new disciples in their faith and gathering them into communities of fervent followers on mission to extend the kingdom.

Cities are the focal point of power, influence and human need. They are the political, economic and intellectual power base of society. If you want to reach the business community, you go to the city. If you want to reach the future leaders of the country, you'll find them studying in the universities of the city. If you want to reach the poor, the oppressed and the exploited masses of society—the groups who are, incidentally, sometimes the most receptive to the gospel—you'll find them in the city.

Cities are filled with masses of hurting people. There are currently thirty megacities in the world in which more than half of the inhabitants live in slums! One billion people worldwide live in shantytowns! And by 2030, the number of slum-dwellers is projected to reach two billion.

Cities contain the highest concentration of virtually every imaginable segment of society, from the most powerful to the most oppressed. The urban population of any major city has the greatest strategic potential for impacting the entire country and the world.

As such, it is reasonable to believe that the city is also the focal point of spiritual warfare. Keller writes, "Because of the power of the city, it is the chief target of the forces of darkness, because that which wins the city sets the course of human life, society and culture.... If the Christian church wants to really change the country and culture, it must go into the cities themselves..."[2]

Another reason why Crossworld believes in the strategic priority of cities is because they afford the greatest potential for disciple-makers from Western cultures to live, work and move among the people without drawing the degree of attention that they would in less populated areas. In a world increasingly hostile to Western culture and closed to faith-based ministry, this is a crucial consideration.

Large urban populations also lend themselves well to the kind of itinerant pioneering ministry that should characterize many of those who are sent to impact the world with the gospel. Western missionary efforts have sometimes taken a settler approach to the task of proclaiming the gospel and making disciples—going to smaller population centers and staying there for decades. While there certainly are situations in which a person is called to spend a lifetime among a small, isolated, unresponsive group of people, the more common biblical pattern is decidedly urban-focused.

The overriding example of Scripture is one of moving among urban populations in search of those in whom the Spirit of God is at work, then proclaiming God's truth, establishing new disciples in their faith, and gathering them into communities of fervent followers on mission to extend the kingdom. The vast urban populations in the world today present an unprecedented opportunity to live and work among millions of people in a single urban area in search of those in whom God is at work.

HOW LONG WOULD IT TAKE?

How long would it take to reach the world if an authentic wave of disciple-makers were launched in all of the nearly five hundred world-class cities of one million or more inhabitants? An infusion of new disciple-makers would invigorate and accelerate what is already going on.

With the roughly forty million evangelical believers that constitute the body of Christ in North America, the hundreds of millions in the body of Christ worldwide, and the hundreds of thousands of faith communities to which they belong, there should be sufficient resources to launch five hundred fresh waves of disciple-makers! Five-hundred teams of disciple-making business entrepreneurs, godly professionals, groundbreakers, ministry leaders and believers from every walk of life could make disciples by imparting God's truth through authentic relationships wherever life happens.

What if we did this not only in the five hundred cities of more than a million people, but in every city of one hundred thousand or more? That's another 2,900 cities. How long would it take to reach the world? If a single believer, reproducing disciple-makers at a rate of one per year, could fill the world with eight billion disciples in just thirty-three years, certainly five hundred waves of disciple-makers spread throughout the world's least-reached marketplaces would transform the world in our lifetime!

Dare I dream such a dream? Would you dream it along with the rest of us at Crossworld? Would you dare to believe, even though in the past two thousand years we have not succeeded in completing Jesus' mandate of discipling all the nations of the world, that we could fully achieve it in our lifetime? I believe we can. I am committed to doing everything possible to make this dream a reality, and Crossworld is looking for people who will join us. Read on as I tell you the stories of individuals who represent the kind of courageous people needed today to forge a better way.

CHAPTER 12

THE KIND OF PEOPLE WHO CHANGE THE WORLD

The best way to reach lost people is by going to their world, not by making them come to ours. It is not by proclaiming the gospel from the safety of our sanctuaries but by incarnating the gospel in their streets and suburbs and slums that we will touch people's hearts.

Monica Starr is a good example of this. Though I am uncertain of her religious convictions, her commitment to making a difference in people's lives is impressive. Her story appeared on the front page of the March 13, 2011, edition of *The Kansas City Star*. As a volunteer for Jackson County Court Appointed Special Advocates, Monica was on a visit to a single mother of five children, all under the age of thirteen. This family's house had virtually no furniture. Not even beds for the children! Her kids slept huddled in a single room, lying on blankets that covered an old, torn carpet.

It was then that Monica's dream for Sleepyhead Beds was born. Her dream was to provide mattresses, box springs and bedding for needy families such as this one. She currently runs this nonprofit out of her own living room and has already provided four hundred beds to area children. She has a waiting list of two hundred more who need a comfortable place to lay their heads at night.[1]

Now let's just imagine that Monica aspires to make an eternal difference in people's lives. Who do you think might have the best chance of impacting those particular families for eternity? Monica Starr or the president of Crossworld? I have the seminary training. I have cross-cultural experience. I have the resources and the proven track record of a great organization. But Monica Starr has their attention. She may even have their hearts because she has taken the time to love them in a very tangible way. If I were a betting man, I'd put my money on Monica Starr.

Wherever Joe goes, he leaves behind him a wake of hope and life. Disciples are made and new communities of faith are born.

Joe is someone else whose life demonstrates the power of living out the gospel in a world of hurting people. Though he lives in Europe, Joe shows up every place a war has erupted because he knows that hurting people offer a unique chance to tangibly model the gospel of love and hope. He was there in Bosnia and Kosovo back in the 1990s before the bullets had stopped flying, bringing in convoys of food, clothing, firewood and anything else that would relieve human suffering.

Not too long after being in Bosnia, war-ravaged Afghanistan came onto Joe's radar. The World Bank had declared that Afghanistan was considered the poorest, most miserable state in the world.[2] This was just the signal Joe needed to go there and establish a beachhead for the gospel through acts of love and mercy.

Wherever Joe goes, he leaves behind him a wake of hope and life. Disciples are made and new communities of faith are born.

Joe more recently set his sights on the remote mountain villages of the Himalayas. What does love look like for a group of people who have a life expectancy of just forty-some years due to deplorable health conditions? Where many die from smoke-induced sickness caused from burning wood inside their huts?

For Joe, part of the answer was to help the fledgling church in that country reach into this totally untouched region with the offer of smokeless stoves and solar panels. Taking teams of young adults and mid-career professionals—physicians, nurses, engineers, managers and technical experts—Joe trekked in solar panels, unassembled stoves, batteries, wires, food, sleeping bags and tents. Christian pastors and evangelists from the city, serving as guides and translators, co-led the teams.

Can you picture it? The team works all day assembling solar panels, wires and lights. Then, at day's end, darkness descends on the village and each family flicks their light switch. And for the first time in history, the village huts are engulfed in light! People cheer and one of the pastors asks the crowd, "How many of you have heard of the Light of the world?" No one responds. And night after night the stories of Jesus are told to these hungry hearts.

Today, two churches are pastored by local believers. More than a hundred people have become disciples of Jesus. They're committed to being discipled and to discipling others. Today a business is emerging from these efforts that will provide employment for people and allow local believers to sustain their outreach to the uttermost parts of that country.

A growing number of villages in that region now have clean cooking, lighting and sanitation solutions that have improved their quality of life. More importantly, in each of the above-mentioned places, God's truth has been shared in the context of life and many have embraced Jesus as a result.

So let me ask you again: Who do you suppose has the best chance of impacting hurting people in places like I've described? A follower of Jesus like Joe, who along with a message of eternal hope gives temporal hope for a better future? Or someone who comes to them with a message of eternal hope that has little real connection to life as they are experiencing it?

To illustrate the power of engaging people where they're living and dying, let me tell you about Samuel Aritan. His story is one of the best examples of the life-transforming potential I've been talking about and to which I aspire.

Samuel is a Middle Eastern businessman whose job requires a significant amount of travel, often to some of the world's most hostile spots. He isn't a particularly religious man, but he's a good man who cares about people. Even though he's caring, he sometimes finds himself on the wrong side of religious fundamentalists who despise people like him—people they consider to have sold out to secularism and capitalism.

One day Sam was on a day trip, traveling between Jerusalem and the occupied West Bank, when he came upon the scene of a man who had been badly assaulted and left for dead along a stretch of road known for its high crime rate. He identified the man as an Israeli. Sam is a Palestinian and has suffered his share of humiliation at the hands of Israeli authorities. But he took the time, at great risk to his own safety, to administer first aid to the man. He brought him to a hotel where he paid for a room and medical care, leaving the hotel owner with a promise to cover any additional costs when he returned.

Perhaps by now you've recognized his story—the ancient story better known as the Good Samaritan (Luke 10:30–37).

What "good Sam Aritan" didn't know was that two religious clerics had arrived on the scene before him and seen the wounded man, but had chosen not to get involved. In fact, they hurried on down *the other side* of the road, as though they'd never seen him.

I don't know how they justified their inaction. It's simply inexcusable that men who were supposed to be in the business of bringing people closer to God were unwilling to get close to people. Perhaps they reasoned that administering first aid was outside their expertise. Or maybe they were in a hurry to do the religious work they were expected to do that day. Did they fear becoming ceremonially unclean if they touched the injured man and he turned out to be dead? Maybe they were just plain scared of getting involved. What is clear, though, is that there was something more important to them than people.

The truth is that people are not impacted by religion. They are impacted by relationship. They are impacted not by our learning, but by our love.

We cannot be sure if the Samaritan man, forever immortalized by Jesus' telling of his story, was a believer in the Christian sense of the word. That was not Jesus' main purpose in telling the story. But let me ask you one more time: Who do you think stood the best chance of making an eternal impact on that Jewish man? If the priest, the Levite and good Sam Aritan wanted to impart spiritual truth to that man, which one would have a window of opportunity with him?

The truth is that people are not impacted by religion. They are impacted by relationship. They are impacted not by our learning, but by our love. They are impacted by those who are willing to cross to their side of the road and experience life where they live and die. And the reality is that the vast majority of people today are living and dying in factories, business towers, restaurants, gas stations and slums—places where people like me have a hard time penetrating, but where people like you are already living.

For most of our eighty years of history, we at Crossworld have defined ourselves as a church-planting mission. We have mobilized predominantly vocational Christian workers who were willing to leave behind career, comfort, family and more in order to preach the gospel and establish churches where Christ was not known.

It was a good vision, a noble vision, a vision worth living and dying for. And God blessed that vision in many ways and places. Places like Haiti, where today there are hundreds of churches and tens of thousands of believers as a result of that vision. Places like the Democratic Republic of Congo, where more than a thousand Crossworld churches live on to this day in spite of decades of war, poverty and one of the worst genocides in modern history. We have done well.

Does that mean we should continue to use the same methods today as we have in the past? We do not continue to travel on ocean freighters to far-flung lands in an age of 747 jets. We do not distribute gospel recordings on hand-cranked phonographs in an age of wireless Internet. We do not light our homes with kerosene lamps in a world of solar and nuclear energy. In a world that is rapidly changing, we cannot rely on what we have done and how we have done it in the past, even if it was very effective at the time.

So in a world where opportunities abound in international business, tourism, education and a multitude of professional disciplines, let's not restrict ourselves to the way we have always done it. In a world where the missionary profession has fallen out of favor with the governments of many least-reached countries, let's open wide the doors for disciple-makers from all professions! In a world of such desperate and massive human need, let's discover the best ways to bring God's truth to their side of the Jericho road.

So today, Crossworld dreams of a new way, a different way, a fresh way. We dream of *disciple-makers from all professions* (the good Sam Aritans of the world) *bringing God's love to life*—crossing the road and tangibly loving people where they're living and dying—using the unique professional and personal skill-sets that God has given them, to impact *the world's least-reached marketplaces.*

In a world of such desperate and massive human need, let's discover the best ways to bring God's truth to their side of the Jericho road.

I am not claiming that this way is better than former ways were in their day. And I'm certainly not claiming that traditional missionaries, such as my wife and I, never really loved people. I am simply saying that if we are to have any hope of discipling the billions of still-to-be-reached people of this world, it will take far more than the religious professional approach of the past. It will take a host of uniquely gifted and courageous men and women who will rise to the challenge in new ways.

CHAPTER 13

FIGHTING TO WIN

Simply stating that there's a better way to reach the world will not make it happen. The longer we are accustomed to doing things one way, the harder it is to forge a new way. For one thing, there is a certain security in maintaining the status quo. It feels safer to keep doing what has always worked, even if it's no longer working so well.

To even suggest that there's a better way can feel like an immediate threat to some. But one of the biggest threats to overcome in forging a new path is not so much the naysayers as it is our own fear of failure. Anyone who is truly committed to overcoming the inertia of *the way we've always done it* needs to have great courage and resolve. Change—even much-needed change—does not come without fighting for it.

I'll admit that I'm not much of a fighter when it comes to fisticuffs. In fact, I can only recall having two fist fights in my entire life, neither of which I wanted. The first one occurred in the fourth grade when I was trying to break up a fight between two boys. Bradley, the aggressor in the fight, suddenly turned on me, and not wanting to get hurt, I decided my best option was to fight back. So with a punch and a kick I knocked him to the ground, sat on him, and continued throwing punches at him. When he began crying, I just had to let him go. I felt so bad that I immediately apologized. I should have known then that I'd never have a career in fighting.

My second fight was a little more serious. It happened after school when two of the tougher boys in my class decided to get even with my friend Jack and me. We had kicked their soccer ball into the weeds earlier that day because they wouldn't let us play with them. So they threatened us with retaliation. And Jack and I were expecting the worst.

When the final school bell sounded, Jack and I high-tailed it out of class and started to sprint home, hoping we'd be able to keep out of Rudy and David's reach. Unfortunately, the distance between school and home was about a mile, and we didn't have enough stamina to outlast Rudy, who also happened to be the fastest runner in our class. We finally managed to duck inside the corner variety store where they couldn't touch us. We stood there, hoping they would get tired of waiting outside and would eventually just go home. After a long while, realizing we couldn't hang out in the store all day, Jack and I raced out of the store prepared to make our last stand.

The only weapon we had was Jack's steel lunchbox. Not wanting to be weaponless, I grabbed a handful of rocks as we bolted from the store. Jack faced off with David, hitting him square in the mouth with his lunchbox. He not only cut David's lip but ruined his own lunchbox.

Rudy, meanwhile, took off after me. Realizing I was not going to outrun him, I turned to face him from about twenty feet away. With a mighty windup, I let my handful of rocks fly in his direction. One of my rocks found its mark and within seconds Rudy had stopped dead in his tracks. With a hand to his mouth, he began yelling through his fingers, "You broke my tooth!" In that instant I knew I had gained a decisive advantage, as well as a window of escape. As Rudy and David assessed the damage, Jack scooped up the scattered contents of his lunch box, and he and I finished our mad dash home—this time without the threat of our pursuers.

That was, unfortunately, not the end of the story. When Rudy and his mother showed up on my doorstep an hour later, I not only had to apologize, but I also had to pay war reparations to help fix his broken tooth.

Thus ended my short but illustrious fighting career.

HOW TO WIN A FIGHT

Though my fighting career only lasted a short time, I did learn a few important principles about fighting to win. The first is a simple principle of wisdom: do whatever you can to avoid a fight, especially if you will most likely lose. As wise King Solomon once wrote, "The beginning of strife is like letting out water, so abandon the quarrel before it breaks out" (Proverbs 17:14).

While the first is a principle of *wisdom,* the second is a principle of *winning*: if you have to fight, fight to win. Half-hearted, fearful fighters rarely win. You cannot win a fight when you're on your heels. You have to be on the balls of your feet leaning into the fight. The very mechanics of the human body dictate that only a forward-leaning stance allows you the mobility needed to fight because the knees and the back were only designed to flex forward, not backward.

So what will it take to fight our way through to a better way of reaching lost people in this rapidly changing world? We see in 1 Samuel 17 what is arguably the best-known fight in the history of the world—the story of David and Goliath. It is universally understood as a picture of triumph in the face of overwhelming odds. It is the story of an entire army of men who were on their heels, while one young man stood on the balls of his feet. But it is far more than that. It is also a picture of Christ, who leads us in victory to live radically different lives.

God made a promise to His people, the Israelites: they would have victory over the Philistines. Despite this promise, Israel was standing on its heels, filled with fear over the Philistine enemy. We are told, "When Saul and all Israel heard these words of the Philistine [Goliath], they were dismayed and greatly afraid" (v. 11). The word *dismayed* comes from a verb that means *to be shattered.* These guys were falling apart with fear.

Amazingly, though, they continued to go through the motions of engaging in battle. They didn't actually *engage* in war, they were just doing war-like motions. Day in and day out for forty days, Goliath would come out to face off with the Israelite soldiers, challenging them to a fight. What did the Israelite fighting men do in response? They would march "out in battle array shouting the war cry" (v. 20). But they never fought or even tried to fight! In fact, on the day David appeared, the army was once again in the process of going through the motions—marching, lining up, chanting war songs and doing nothing.

They had a bigger view of the opposition than they had of God.

I can just imagine their chant. Perhaps it went something like this: "Wake up soldier, out of bed... Philistines are good as dead... We don't tremble, we don't flinch... We'll take this country inch by inch...." To which any intelligent observer would have responded, "Yeah, right."

These soldiers had no intention of fighting. In fact, the Bible tells us, "When all the men of Israel saw the man, they fled from him and were greatly afraid" (v. 24).

What was wrong with these guys? One obvious answer is that they had a bigger view of the opposition than they had of God. We'll talk about that in a moment. But notice another problem that we tend to overlook: Israel had allowed the enemy to define the terms of the battle. What were those terms? A one-on-one contest with a giant in a classic battle of strength and weaponry. I don't know who had agreed to these terms, but for some reason everyone seemed to go along with them.

What's more, King Saul's approach to a losing battle was absolutely useless. He offered all kinds of incentives to the person who was brave enough to fight against the giant. He was giving away tax-free status and even the hand of his daughter in marriage! Wow! I wonder why there were no takers. Probably because it's hard to show up for your wedding when you're dead! When you're fighting on your heels in a battle where you're out-gunned and the enemy has made all the rules, trying to increase people's motivation is the wrong approach.

GOLIATH VS. THE MISSIONARY ENDEAVOR

There are some interesting parallels between what Israel was facing then and what the church is facing today in its global mandate.

The church in the West is on its heels in the battle for human souls. In spite of the apparent robustness of the megachurch movement in North America, the church is losing ground. Virtually every study on the health of the evangelical movement in the West shows a church that is losing its youth, not making disciples and having little visible impact on society.

Dr. Richard Krejcir of the Schaeffer Institute observes that "from 1990 to 2000, the combined membership of all Protestant denominations in the USA declined by almost 5 million members (9.5 percent), while the US population increased by 24 million (11 percent)."[1]

According to George Barna of the Barna Group, North America is the only continent in the world today where the church is not growing. He compares it to the Titanic, describing it as "large, elegant, and sinking fast."[2]

And faced with such daunting realities in a world that seems increasingly hostile to their message, the church and the missionary enterprise, like the Israelites of old, don't know what to do.

The missionary endeavor of the Western church is also struggling. Missionary dollars are becoming more difficult to find. Church missions budgets are downsizing. Annual mission conferences are shortened. Missionary careers are gradually becoming a thing of the past. An increasing number of missionary-sending organizations are in a battle for survival. And faced with such daunting realities in a world that seems increasingly hostile to their message, the church and the missionary enterprise, like the Israelites of old, don't know what to do.

Yet, like Saul's army, they keep going through the motions—marching in and out of the church building once a week, singing the battle hymns of the faith. Once a year they set aside a Sunday to decorate their camp with the flags of the spiritual prisoners they talk about liberating. As morale drops, they try to fire up the troops with their most inspiring spokesmen who paint pictures of the dire condition of the lost world. Once in a while they bring in a soldier from the front lines to tell stories from the war zone. They honor him on a Sunday evening with a potluck and a small gathering of mostly older folks they call "prayer warriors," and he tells a few of his stories before they send him off again. They talk about the battle, pray about the battle, sing about the battle, but for the most part, they are desperately afraid to engage in the battle.

As for the terms of engagement, many have allowed the enemy to define the way the battle must be fought. Only religious professionals are allowed to do battle—only if they are spiritual giants and successful fund-raisers and do full-time religious kinds of things, and only once they've gone through a lengthy, mostly academic training regimen.

Thankfully this does not describe the entire church in the West. There are some wonderful disciple-making, innovative, globally focused ministries out there that are engaging in the battle with faith and courage. But they are not the majority. Many church and mission endeavors today resemble Saul and his army. They're on their heels and going through the motions.

FIGHTING FORWARD

We need men and women who can change the momentum of the battle—men and women who, by faith, will lean into the battle using their God-given uniqueness and fight in ways the enemy least expects. Men and women like David and like Christ Himself. How did David change the momentum in the fight against Goliath?

First of all, he *redefined the terms of engagement*, falling back on a simpler, more ancient approach to fighting: the stone and the sling. Goliath had defined the terms of battle as a one-on-one classic battle of strength and weaponry. Saul had bought into those terms, and when this hapless young lad named David stepped forward, Saul actually tried to fit him into the same traditional box by dressing him in *his own* armor! Fortunately, David graciously declined the offer and opted to redefine the battle in terms that he understood—using a shepherd's staff and a sling as his weapons rather than heavy armor.

In a similar way, Jesus challenged the traditions of His day and redefined the terms of engagement, refusing to be forced into the traditions of the religious "experts" who tied up heavy loads and laid them on men's shoulders (Matthew 23:4).

But challenging the status quo and redefining the terms of engaging the battle is not easy. It wasn't easy for David, it certainly wasn't easy for Jesus, and it still isn't easy today. It can be intimidating and lonely, not to mention downright dangerous.

In their book *Blue Ocean Strategy*, authors W. Chan Kim and Renee Mauborgne contrast *red oceans*—the well-charted world of business where most companies go head to head with each other in an over-crowded sea of competitors—with *blue oceans*—the untapped market space that relatively few discover because of the tendency to stick with the pack and do things the way we've always done them.[3]

When David stepped onto the battlefield with a stone and a sling, he stepped into a huge patch of blue ocean. Everyone else was jockeying for position in the red ocean of traditional warfare, and David found himself all alone.

Blue ocean can be intimidating for the simple fact that you find yourself all alone. What if I'm wrong? If this is such a great idea, why am I the only one to have thought of it or tried it? But blue ocean is also exhilarating because it leaves you free to sail and discover things you never would have by sticking with the pack.

If we are going to win the battle for the souls of men and women today, we are going to have to find some blue ocean. It may be comforting to sail around in red ocean with everyone else, knowing that you're not alone. But comforting inertia is not acceptable in the battle for lost souls. I will admit that, as the leader of Crossworld, I am nervous about the prospect of blue ocean. But I have decided that I would rather fail in an exhilarating quest for the lost than succeed in going through the motions.

FIGHTING FROM A POSITION OF STRENGTH

The second thing David did to change the momentum was to *fight from his strength*. He had no experience tromping around in body armor and throwing spears, but he was one incredible stone-slinger. So that's what he did. Yet it was not his sling that was his strength. David's sling was actually a symbol of weakness or foolishness—thus the taunts of the enemy. And he was not trusting in his sling, for he clearly said, "The LORD does not deliver by sword or by spear" (he could have easily added *or by sling*), "for the battle is the LORD's!" (1 Samuel 17:47). *That* was his position of strength—not a sword, a spear or even a sling, but allowing God to do battle by pouring His strength through the weakness of who he was and what he had to offer.

I have decided that I would rather fail in an exhilarating quest for the lost than succeed in going through the motions.

So it was with the cross of Christ—a stumbling block to the Jews and foolishness to the Gentiles, "but to those who are the called…Christ the power of God and the wisdom of God. Because the foolishness of God is wiser than men, and the weakness of God is stronger than men" (1 Corinthians 1:23-25).

I do not understand why we have for so long handicapped the missionary effort by making godly believers lay aside their "slings" to take up our so-called "swords and spears" to go and do battle "the missionary way." Like Saul, we try to make others fit into our armor. But lost humanity desperately needs godly engineers and baristas, electricians and web designers, business entrepreneurs and more to flood the marketplaces of the world with their best skills, so that disciples of Jesus can be made wherever life happens.

When we ask people to abandon their God-given skills and passions to become full-time religious workers, or when we tell people to just send money and the "missionaries" will take care of the Great Commission, we are doing ourselves and the lost world a great disservice.

A HIGHER MOTIVATION

Saul's response to a losing battle was to try and increase his troops' motivation, namely by giving money and his daughter's hand. But even a lifetime tax break and becoming the king's son-in-law could not get a single soldier to step out of the ranks and fight. These men may have been frightened, but they were not stupid!

The only thing that will move a man or woman to abandon the relative security of merely going through the motions is a passion for the honor and fame of the living God.

What launched David into the battle was a much higher motivation—that of God's glory. It is intriguing to note that not a single soldier, Saul included, mentioned God. They talked a lot about the giant: "Have you seen this man who is coming up? Surely he is coming up to defy Israel" (1 Samuel 17:25). And they talked about the reward: "The king will enrich the man who kills him with great riches…" (v. 25). But only David talked about his God: "For who is this uncircumcised Philistine, that he should taunt the armies of the living God?" (v. 26). While the soldiers saw Goliath's threat as an assault against the army of Israel, David saw it as an assault against *the God* of the army of Israel!

Do you recall what motivated Jesus the night before going to the cross and dealing a death blow to the enemy? It was a passion for God's glory! "Father, the hour has come; glorify Your Son, that the Son may glorify You.... This is eternal life, that they may know You.... I glorified You on the earth, having accomplished the work which You have given Me to do..." (John 17:1–4).

Personal or financial security is a miserable motivator when it comes to engaging in a life-and-death battle. The only thing that will move a man or woman to abandon the relative security of merely going through the motions is a passion for the honor and fame of the living God.

FIGHTING THE GOOD FIGHT OF FAITH

The last and most important game changer for David was his faith in God. The old hymn by John Yates says it perfectly: "Faith is the victory that overcomes the world."[4] David believed God, plain and simple. He believed what God had said when He promised the land to Israel. He believed what God had said about driving out its wicked inhabitants. He believed that God's honor was being insulted. And he believed that God could use a shepherd boy and his sling to change the momentum.

And that's exactly what happened. The momentum of that little stone and the faith behind it was like a gust of wind in the backs of the men of Israel, pushing them from their heels to the balls of their feet so that they "arose and shouted and pursued the Philistines as far the valley, and to the gates of Ekron" (1 Samuel 17:52). No longer were they shouting the meaningless chants that had characterized the previous forty days of their cowering existence. But they were shouting gut-wrenching cries of victory!

Oh, that God may once again fill His people with shouts of victory! He can do it. And He can use you to do it. It only took one boy filled with God to launch an entire army into a battle they should have already been fighting. One boy, one stone, and one powerful God defeated an enemy that had only moments earlier looked impossible to beat.

And did you notice the exclamation mark He put on the event? The text says of Goliath, "The stone sank into his forehead, so that he fell on his face to the ground" (1 Samuel 17:49). Why did God specify that Goliath fell "on his face"? It sounds a bit like a position of worship, doesn't it? The statement is reminiscent of another account in 1 Samuel where a Philistine god found himself in the same position—face-down before the God of Israel. In that story, the ark of God had been captured by the Philistines and placed in the temple of Dagon. In the morning when the worshippers arrived, they found that "Dagon had fallen on his face to the ground before the ark of the LORD" (1 Samuel 5:4). Not only that, the same verse says that he had also lost his head and his hands in the process so that "only the trunk of Dagon was left to him."

Oh, that God may once again fill His people with shouts of victory! He can do it. And He can use you to do it.

Is it not interesting that both Dagon and Goliath found themselves face down with their heads severed from their bodies when they dared to take on the God of Israel? In both cases, the point is inescapable: God will not share His glory with man or idol. All will ultimately bow before Him and He will be worshipped.

God is in the business of being glorified, and He wants to use people like you to make it happen. The battle for the souls of mankind is a fight we cannot walk away from. The enemy has, for much too long, defined the terms of battle, insulted our God and put us on our heels. It's time to lean forward in faith, believing that God made us with our unique skills and passions because He wants to use them to win battles for His glory. There is so much blue ocean out there and so few people sailing in it. I want to be one of them. How about you?

by LARRY SHARP, Crossworld's Vice President for Business Partnerships

CHAPTER 14

CHARTING A NEW COURSE

Blue ocean is a beautiful and frightening thing all at the same time. When viewed from the relative safety of a cruise liner, it is undeniably beautiful. On the other hand, to be surrounded by thousands of miles of blue ocean with nothing but a small sailboat between me and the bottom of it is a thought that scares me beyond words.

Consequently, I have a hard time understanding what motivates people like Laura Dekker. On January 21, 2012, this sixteen-year-old became the youngest person to sail alone around the globe. She did it in a thirty-eight-foot sailboat named Guppy, covering more than twenty-seven thousand nautical miles.[1]

I find that hard to comprehend. It's one thing to sail around the globe on a cruise ship with hundreds of other passengers. It's quite another to brave the danger, loneliness and elements alone in a boat that could easily be swallowed by waves twice its size.

So what motivates us in our pursuit of a better way to reach lost people with the gospel? Why not continue to sail in the well-charted waters of the missionary endeavors of the past century that, in many cases, have served us well? I can assure you that it is not for the sake of adventure. Nor do we think that we're the only ones in a vast blue ocean who are willing to attempt something new.

We, and others like us, are driven by a desire to see Jesus known and worshipped everywhere. And we are driven by a conviction that the only way the Great Commission can be accomplished in our lifetime is if all believers from all professions will flood the world's least-reached marketplaces as incarnational disciple-makers.

Yet many aspects of how that dream can be realized are yet to be discovered. I will be the first to admit that we are far from figuring it all out. In a very real sense, it is uncharted blue ocean. And that's what scares me. But I agree with what Dale wrote previously: I would rather fail in an exhilarating quest for lost souls than succeed in simply going through the motions.

We have much to learn and we are learning much! And we're looking for people with a disciple-making heart to join us in the journey. Let me tell you about some who have followed our dream to give you a better picture of what the realization of this dream could look like.

MODERN MODELS

On the Assembly Line

Jon and Judy live and serve in an unreached East Asian country. Most people there do not know about, let alone follow, Jesus. After serving there for two years as quasi missionaries and finding it difficult to stay long term, Jon and Judy wondered and prayed about finding *a better way* to impact the people they had been reaching out to.

Jon realized he had an entrepreneurial mind and that he could use it to gain long-term access to Asia. Jon's business bent and heart for the Great Commission and Judy's spiritual gift of evangelism and her passion for sharing Jesus seemed to be a perfect combination for reaching people through business. They developed a business idea, created a business plan and found two investors. Before long, Jon and Judy were back in Asia and a small factory was born.

The *quadruple bottom line* [of BAM] means that the business needs to (1) be profitable and sustainable, (2) create community value and local jobs, (3) make followers of Jesus, and (4) promote environmental stewardship.

It was not easy for them to run a business, but they were driven by the calling of God to make disciples in the workplace. The *quadruple bottom line* of Business as Mission (BAM) was also a tremendous motivation for their work. The quadruple bottom line means that the business needs to (1) be profitable and sustainable, (2) create community value and local jobs, (3) make followers of Jesus, and (4) promote environmental stewardship.

The road to success is usually long and arduous, and it certainly was for Jon and Judy. But today their business is profitable! People from both the employee pool and from relationships in the community have come to know Jesus and are being discipled.

Jon and Judy certainly qualify as "missionaries"—disciple-making "sent ones"—but being a missionary is not legal in their country. It is, however, perfectly legal to own a business, provide jobs for thirty employees, and live like Jesus. And that is exactly what they are doing—to the making of disciples who are, in turn, making other disciples, and to the greater glory of God.

Coffee Anyone?

Becky is another example. She graduated from a university with a degree in international business and had worked at Starbucks for several years, learning a lot about the coffee industry. But Becky was more than a rising businesswoman. She wanted Jesus' name to be known and disciples to multiply in places where there are few believers.

She joined Crossworld, and in partnership with a like-minded organization, was sent to a former Soviet republic in Asia. Years ago we would have asked Becky to "give up her skills for Jesus." But not today! The call to the Beckys of the world is to "use it all up" rather than "give it all up." And that is exactly what Becky decided to do.

In this impoverished country with high unemployment and poverty rates, the level of desperation caused people to ask Becky questions such as, "Why is America rich and we are poor? What is it like in your country?" Though the answers are complex, Becky and her team knew that the best way to answer these questions, build trust and share a greater message of hope was to connect with their lives. So they looked for a way to offer a service to the community.

Soon a business plan emerged, and God supplied the capital to start a coffee business in this country with little history of coffee. Becky reasoned something like this: if they want to learn about America, they need to learn English and learn to drink coffee. The business plan and financial projections included the importation of coffee beans, coffee roasters, grinders and all the other sorts of equipment needed to put coffee on the market and in the cup of the tea drinkers in that country.

After years of prayer, hard work and God's hand of blessing, the business idea came to fruition. Today there are two Starbucks-like coffee shops in the capital city. The businesses are profitable and sustainable with employees. Most importantly, there are people living and loving like Jesus and imparting God's truth through authentic relationships where life happens—the coffee shop! Disciples are following Jesus and multiplying in their community.

Most importantly, there are people living and loving like Jesus and imparting God's truth through authentic relationships where life happens—the coffee shop!

Float Your Boat

A few years ago, Andrew called the Crossworld office to talk to the vice president responsible for BAM. Andrew was a missionary in Asia, and although he was an architect by training, he had started two churches using his boat to visit remote islands. He now wanted help in buying a small factory that was for sale in an unreached area.

Andrew loved Jesus, knew how to make disciples, loved the outdoors, and knew how to build stuff. But he had never owned and operated a for-profit business.

So it was that several business consultants with disciple-making hearts set to work. They provided Andrew financial due diligence, opened contracts with legal and accounting authorities in the country, developed a business and marketing plan, gave counsel for raising the necessary capital, and helped him build a ministry plan. Before long the business was his.

But how does a business with twenty-five employees, devoted to making a profit and creating much-needed jobs, really make disciples of Jesus?

Andrew asked himself that same question. He asked others for help. And most importantly, he asked daily for God's help and wisdom.

For Andrew, the answer laid in living out the gospel every day by being fair with employees, paying his taxes, paying a fair wage, placing verses from the book of Proverbs on the office door and starting the day in prayer for everyone (even the Muslim and Hindu employees). It involved building relationships, caring for the families, and even weekend camping trips with the employees. It meant talking about the real issues of life and showing them who Jesus is and how a follower of His really lives. Some call it *discipling people into the kingdom*—or discipleship before the cross.

We recently received the following message from Andrew: "A fifty-six-year-old Muslim man just accepted the Lord and was baptized yesterday! He has a wife and two twenty-something boys. He is a changed man, and even his wife can see it. Please pray for him and his family, as I understand his wife will seek approval from her family to follow his 'new faith' in Jesus."

Andrew is now discipling an employee on the other side of the cross and continues to trust God for many more. He is experiencing the quadruple bottom line of doing BAM. And he's accomplishing Jesus' Great Commission to make disciples by obeying Jesus' Great Commandments to love God supremely and to love people sacrificially.

How Did It Happen?

These stories, representative of many others like them, may appear almost simplistic and surreal. Let me assure you that they did not happen without much prayer, planning and hard work. What was needed to make them happen?

Jon and Judy needed people who were willing to take a chance, invest in their business, and believe it could make a difference in the hearts of people who had never heard the good news. They needed a financial professional to mentor them in a simple financial software. They also needed two business professionals to help them do the background work needed to qualify for a loan.

These are the kind of brave men and women we are looking for to help us sail the uncharted blue ocean of the world in which we live.

Becky needed people in the coffee industry to assist her in developing a business plan and obtaining venture capital. She also needed a marketing expert to advise her on how to promote her coffeeshop.

All of these people were already 925ers. They had been living out the gospel in their own workplace, making it more natural to transplant their work expertise and passion for the gospel into a new culture.

These are the kind of brave men and women we are looking for to help us sail the uncharted blue ocean of the world in which we live. These are the kind of people whose diverse professional skills will allow us to penetrate the world's least-reached marketplaces that are increasingly difficult to enter by traditional means. These are the people we need to come alongside the seminary-trained workers like myself to innovatively discover ways to impact people where they are living and dying.

THE WHOLE BODY OF BELIEVERS AND THEIR ROLES

What I have shared is a dream, but it is more than a dream. It is a mandate that is rooted in the very heart of God and His Word and is demonstrated in both biblical and world history. The *better way* is not a new way; it is God's way. It's Jesus' way of transforming the world. Jesus' way is disciple-makers, not converts. Jesus' way is living a message of abundant life, not simply preaching a message of eternal life. And Jesus' way involves all of His followers, not just a select few.

Take a look at some of the following roles that need to be filled today if we are to achieve the dream. Then ask yourself the question: "Where do I fit?"

International Disciple-Makers

Ground-breakers are pioneers who are ready to be agents of change. They enter a new least-reached marketplace ahead of the rest of the team to seek out solid job opportunities and strategies for the team members who will follow. They lead toward new ideas, methods, directions and opportunities, and follow God courageously in the breaking of new ground. They are determined to make disciples on the spiritual frontiers. Joe, whose story we told in Chapter 12, is one such man.

Business developers are men and women who have the ability and experience to develop profitable and sustainable business opportunities that fit a particular marketplace. They create community value through job creation, social justice or community development. The community value they bring makes them highly desirable, even in restricted-access countries. They have exceptional business, human resource or leadership skills and have proven themselves to understand how these skills integrate with living out kingdom values in the workplace. They strive for results and are accountable for both the business and the making of disciples. Jon, Judy and Becky are business developers.

Profession-based disciple-makers are people who will take a job in their area of expertise as a means of establishing placement and credibility in the least-reached marketplace. They can be medical professionals, engineers, IT experts, sports professionals, linguists, teachers or music/culture experts. Their skill is marketable with an international company, an NGO working abroad or with a business startup. Though they are tentmakers or self-employed, they create value in the domain of their profession, demonstrating God's love by making disciples of Jesus. They establish themselves through integrity, credibility and sustainability. My anesthesiologist friend has taken professional opportunities in two unreached countries of the 10/40 Window. He's a profession-based disciple-maker who loves Jesus and wants more people following Him.

Ministry team leaders are people who help keep the team focused on and accountable for the goal of reproducing disciple-makers. They have strengths in pastoring, teaching or member care. They provide servant-leadership, coordination skills and team-building accountability, all the while pursuing full-life transformation of the people with whom they are in contact.

Vocational cross-cultural workers are people whose experience and training lend itself to a more focused attention on the spiritual development of team members and new disciples. They may be referred to as traditional missionaries. They focus on developing leaders so that local communities of believers (churches) will grow and multiply. There is still a great need for vocational cross-cultural workers to bring God's love to the unreached!

North American-Based Disciple-Makers

Recruiters and networkers are people who catch the vision—who see the impact of engaging the entire body of Christ to use their gifts, talents and experience to impact the unreached. They have respected voices in their circles and are able to inspire those around them. Business people and professionals understand what it's like to recruit and be recruited; they get what it means to network. They are the ones who cast vision, share their passion, and draw others to join them in bringing hope to the far ends of the earth.

Business/professional mentors are people with proven business or professional skills who can mentor younger people just entering their profession. Those who desire to use their business and professional skills to serve God internationally need mentors, especially if they are young. They need to see how faith is lived out in the workplace of their profession, and they need experienced professionals here in North America to help them develop their professional skills before seeking to implement them cross-culturally.

Intern developers are business owners or professional workers who hire interns to provide them with real-life work experience. This will prepare them not only for their profession, but also for an integrated understanding of faith in their marketplace. Intern developers usually do this with younger, less-experienced workers. The internship can be somewhat formal, perhaps connected to a university program. The ultimate goal remains the same—the intern desires to understand how to live life in the workplace and take his or her profession to the unreached world.

Business start-up sponsors are people who have access to financial assets and understand how these funds can be used for kingdom purposes. They are willing to contribute start-up capital by making a loan or by taking an equity position in the start-up business. They may be willing to fund a person going overseas for one to five years. Or they may wish to donate to the start-up business or professional endeavor. Financial investors, donors or loan-makers may connect with individuals directly or through an approved ministry project fund to accomplish the same end goal: making disciples through their profession in the world's least-reached marketplaces.

Consultants or *coaches* are men and women who, from their current position in North America (or elsewhere), are able to coach a businessperson or a start-up professional endeavor overseas. They often serve as a Subject Matter Expert (SME) or as a general consultant, helping to determine what is needed. Lisa was a former product developer for a Fortune 500 company, and she now works from home helping BAM startups to refine their product for the consumer. Ken, a former corporate executive, worked from his home in Pennsylvania to help Andrew qualify for his business loan. Rick is mentoring a new start-up water project in an Asian country he recently visited.

CONCLUSION

We at Crossworld are charting a new course, and we need your help. We need people from all walks of life to help us discover the better way to impact our rapidly changing world—people who will pray with us, dream with us, plan with us, share their expertise and resources with us, and go with us. We cannot discover the better way alone. But with God's help and the wisdom He has entrusted to the whole body of Christ, we will discover it.

Remember Dale's story about his son Joel at the beginning of this book? Joel's desire to impact the world for Jesus using the skills

We at Crossworld are charting a new course, and we need your help. ... We cannot discover the better way alone. But with God's help and the wisdom He has entrusted to the whole body of Christ, we will discover it.

and passions God has given to him is a desire that is shared by many believers the world over. It is a God-given desire born out of a conviction that Jesus' great disciple-making mandate is for every one of His followers.

It is our deep longing and prayer that the millions of Christians like

Joel will rise up and, by faith, dare to believe that God will use them to shake the nations and stir His people for His eternal glory. God will be worshipped—of that you can be sure. And He invites *you* to be part of making it happen.

RESTRICTED ACCESS COUNTRIES AND THEIR POPULATIONS

Restricted access countries*	Population
Afghanistan	29,835,392
Algeria	34,994,937
Azerbaijan	8,372,373
Bahrain	1,214,705
Bangladesh	158,570,535
Belarus	9,577,552
Bhutan	708,427
Brunei	401,890
China and Tibet	1,336,718,015
Comoros	794,683
Cuba	11,087,330
Egypt	82,079,636
Eritrea	5,939,484
Ethiopia	90,873,739
Gaza and the West Bank	4,225,710
India	1,189,172,906
Indonesia	245,613,043
Iran	77,891,220
Iraq	30,399,572
Jordan	6,508,271
Kazakhstan	15,522,373
Kuwait	2,595,628
Kyrgyzstan	5,587,443
Laos	6,477,211
Lebanon	4,143,101

*Excludes countries without official persecution, such as Mexico.

Sources: The Voice of the Martyrs, July 11, 2007; Central Intelligence Agency, The World Factbook (2007), citing estimates from July 2011

Used by Permission of The Voice of the Martyrs (www.persecution.com).

Restricted access countries	Population
Libya	6,597,960
Malaysia	28,728,607
Maldives	394,999
Mauritania	3,281,634
Morocco	31,968,361
Myanmar	53,999,804
Nepal	29,391,883
Nigeria	155,215,573
North Korea	24,457,492
Oman	3,027,959
Pakistan	187,342,721
Qatar	848,016
Saudi Arabia	26,131,703
Somalia	9,925,640
Sri Lanka	21,283,913
Sudan	45,047,502
Syria	22,517,750
Tajikistan	7,627,200
Tunisia	10,629,186
Turkey	78,785,548
Turkmenistan	4,997,503
United Arab Emirates	5,148,664
Uzbekistan	28,128,600
Vietnam	90,549,390
Yemen	24,133,492
Total Population	**4,259,466,276**

Note: The current world population is 6,928,198,253 (July 2011 estimate) and 61.48 percent are in restricted access countries.

NOTES

CHAPTER 3

The Holy Bible, King James Version (New York: Oxford Edition, 1769); see also http://www.kingjamesbibleonline.org.

Henry Wace and C. A. Bucheim, eds., *Luther's Primary Works* (London: Hodder and Stoughton, 1896), 401.

Dorothy Sayers, *Creed or Chaos* (Bedford, NH: Sophia Institute Press, 1995), 56. Quoted by Doug Sherman in *Your Work Matters to God* (Colorado Springs: NavPress, 1990), 20.

William Carr Peel and Walt Larimore, MD, *Going Public With Your Faith* (Grand Rapids: Zondervan, 2003).

CHAPTER 4

Rick Wood, "The Key to Discipling all Peoples," *Mission Frontiers*, January/February 2011, 4.

Bill Hull, *Jesus Christ: Disciplemaker* (Grand Rapids: Baker Books, 2004), 10.

Bill Hull, *The Complete Book of Discipleship* (Colorado Springs: NavPress, 2006), 16–17.

Dietrich Bonhoeffer, *The Cost of Discipleship* (New York: Macmillan, 1937), 64.

CHAPTER 5

"Man Pledges to End the Slaughter of the Ghosts of Tanzania," *National Post*, February 28, 2009.

Commonly attributed by English language dictionaries to Josef Stalin; first appeared in a 1958 book review in the *New York Times*.

Robert Coleman, *The Master Plan of Discipleship* (Grand Rapids: Fleming H. Revell, 1998), 15.

Lewis Sperry Chafer, *True Evangelism: Winning Souls Through Prayer* (Grand Rapids: Kregel Publications, 1993), 58.

CHAPTER 6

Josh McDowell, *The Disconnected Generation* (Nashville: Thomas Nelson, 2000), 29.

CHAPTER 7

Philip Schaff, ed., *Creeds of Christiandom*, Vol. 3 (New York: Cosmio, repr. 2007), 611.

Michael Gungor, "Untangling the Gramophone," *Christianity Today*, last modified February 9, 2012, accessed February 13, 2012, http://www.christianitytoday.com/ct/music/commentaries/2012/untanglinggramophone.html?start=1.

CHAPTER 8

Tim Keller, *Redeemer Church Planting Manual* (New York: Redeemer Presbyterian Church, 2009), 46.

Ibid.

CHAPTER 9

Dorothy Sayers, *Creed or Chaos*, (Bedford, NH: Sophia Institute Press, 1995), 56. Quoted by Doug Sherman in *Your Work Matters to God* (Colorado Springs: NavPress, 1990), 20.

R.G. Le Tourneau, *Mover of Men and Mountains* (Chicago: Moody Press, 1967).

Michael Metzger, "Dilemmas and Distortions," *DoggieHeadTilt* (blog), February 9, 2007, http://www.doggieheadtilt.com/dilemmas-and-distortions.

Jay Lorenzen, "Amazing Grace: The Story of William Wilberforce," *On-Movements* (blog), February 10, 2007, http://onmovements.com/?p=188.

David Platt, *Radical Together* (Colorado Springs: Multnomah Books, 2011), 10.

CHAPTER 10

Bill Hull, *Jesus Christ: Disciplemaker* (Grand Rapids: Baker Books, 2004), 9.

Bob Roberts, "We Aren't About Weekends," *Leadership Journal*, posted January 1, 2007, http://www.christianitytoday.com/le/2007/winter/3.28.

CHAPTER 12

Laura Bauer, "Fairway Woman's Nonprofit Gives Needy Kids a Place to Sleep," *The Kansas City Star*, March 13, 2011.

The World Bank, Report on Afghanistan, October 2001.

CHAPTER 13

Richard Krejcir, "Statistics and Reasons for Church Decline." Schaeffer Institute, 2007, http://www.intothyword.org/articles_view.asp?articleid=36557.

George Barna, *The Second Coming of the Church* (Nashville: Word Publishing, 1997), 8.

W. Chan Kim and Renee Mauborgne, *Blue Ocean Strategy* (Boston: Harvard Business School Press, 2005).

John Yates, "Faith Is the Victory," *Celebration Hymnal* (Word Music/Integrity Music, 1997), 727.

CHAPTER 14

Judy Fitzpatrick, "Teen Ends Globe-Circling Voyage in St. Maarten," *Associate Press*, January 21, 2012.

ABOUT THE AUTHOR

Born and raised in Ontario, Canada, Dale Losch (*lawsh*) trusted Christ as Savior at the age of six. He received his bachelor's degree in Missions in 1981 from Christian Heritage College in El Cajon, California. He received his master's degree in Theology in 1987 from Dallas Theological Seminary in Dallas, Texas. He married Jerusha in 1982 and they have four children: Joel, Jessica, Nathan and Hannah.

In 1988, after three years in pastoral ministry in North America, Dale and Jerusha went to France to serve with Crossworld. After nine years of ministry there, they left an established church under national leaderhsip and returned to Canada where Dale became the Canadian Director of Crossworld. In January 2009, Dale became President of Crossworld.

Today, Dale writes, speaks and preaches on the topics of discipleship, missions and God's heart for the world. Jerusha is a teacher by profession and enjoys extending the gift of hospitality. Dale and Jerusha make their home in Kansas City, Mo.